Instructor's Resource Manual

Master Student Guide to Academic Success

Robert Onorato
Sacred Heart University

HOUGHTON MIFFLIN COMPANY BOSTON NEW YORK

Publisher: Patricia A. Coryell
Senior Sponsoring Editor: Mary Finch
Development Editor: Shani B. Fisher
Editorial Associate: Andrew Sylvester
Senior Manufacturing Coordinator: Florence Cadran
Marketing Manager: Elinor Gregory

Printed in the U.S.A.

ISBN: 0-618-38257-7

123456789-QD-08 07 06 05 04

Table of Contents

Introduction: Explanation of Concept

The *Master Student Guide to Academic Success* has been written and designed to help students succeed in one of the most important endeavors that they will ever undertake: their college careers. The execution of this journey is not always easy, yet its navigation and successful completion can determine the course of a student's life for years to come. Whether making the transition from high school to college student to working professional or balancing the conflicting demands of family, work, and school, students often need advice, direction, and support. We hope *The Master Student Guide* will help to provide these. In addition, you, as an instructor, teacher, or professor, can play an important role in guiding and supporting a student through this undertaking. *The Master Student Guide* can be one of the tools that you use to help your students to successfully accomplish their academic journeys.

The *Guide* provides a unique structure and features to help students and professors achieve these goals. The book is tabbed throughout, and each tab provides students with a quick summary or reference of the key concepts introduced in the corresponding chapter. This allows students to find the topics they are searching for easily. In addition, this tabbed page can serve students as a review sheet to brush up on material without having to read an entire chapter. Each chapter also contains checklists that provide students with places to interact with the text, allowing them to participate as active learners in the new concepts that they have studied. Further, frequent sidebars and examples are used throughout the text to provide students with additional ways to apply these skills throughout their college courses and in other areas of their lives. Examples of sidebars include: Ways to Set Priorities (Chapter 6); Ways to Evaluate Your Notes (Chapter 15); and Reduce Fear of Public Speaking (Chapter 25). Finally, students are encouraged to apply the skills from each chapter directly to other courses they are taking as well as to their own lives through "Experiment with a Strategy from This Chapter." This excellent resource is found at the end of each chapter. Students are encouraged to complete these exercises in the space provided in the text. These features allow you and your students to tailor this book to the unique needs of your courses and their lives. As a result, the *Master Student Guide* can be used as a main textbook, ancillary supporting book, primary resource support, or reference guide. You can choose to cover all of the chapters or quickly and easily select the ones that most directly relate to the needs of your classroom situation.

Although the primary focus of the lives of college students is, or should be, academics, most students cannot shut out all of the other parts of their lives in order to concentrate only on their academic success. Many students will be away from their homes and families for the first times in their lives. They may feel lonely or insecure. Many students will have to work while in school. Some students may have families to support or care for. They must try to balance these conflicting demands on their valuable time. Some students may face social pressure to participate in unhealthy or dangerous behaviors. In addition, students may experience a volume and/or level of academic work that is new to them. The simple management of time and balance of conflicting demands can be difficult challenges for them to overcome.

Therefore, *The Master Student Guide to Academic Success* addresses a student's academic success in the context of the whole student. Though the *Guide* develops skills in the traditional areas of note-taking (Chapters 11–15), outlining (Chapter 14), active reading (Chapter 9), research (Chapters 20–21), test-taking (Chapters 18–19), and many other essential topics, it also examines decision-making (Chapter 5), creative idea generation (Chapter 4), learning styles and cycles (Chapter 2), successful student interaction (Chapters 1–2), as well as many others. In addition, as *The Master Student Guide* explains and teaches its lessons, it is cognizant of the fact that if a student is healthy, he can learn better and more efficiently. It understands that a student who is not distracted can focus more fully.

It knows that it is normal to feel overwhelmed sometimes in college or to have low self-confidence in the face of a subject that is difficult to master. The *Guide* understands that a student who believes in herself can achieve more.

As you and your students work toward their academic success, the *Guide* attempts to teach yet at the same time enable students to understand that life seldom presents the ideal environment and conditions for academic discipline. While *The Master Student Guide* presents the academic skills needed for success in college, it also hopes to help students understand that conflicting priorities will be encountered, multiple demands will be made on their time, less than ideal influences will be met, and unhealthy habits will be developed. Yet it offers guidance to overcome all of these challenges, maintain focus on study and course work, and ultimately achieve success in one's chosen area of study.

Finally, while the primary focus of *The Master Student Guide to Academic Success* is the achievement of success in the student's pursuit of higher education, it is understood that the skills and strategies developed to meet these challenges can also provide both professional and personal benefits. It is from this viewpoint that the *Guide* is written. It makes frequent reference to the benefits of a healthy, well-adjusted personal life and to the advantages gained by a responsible, organized, and well-managed professional life. The *Guide* never focuses only on college life. It hopes to convince students that the strategies, skills, and habits that are outlined and taught within its chapters will help students in all areas of their lives. For example, when strategies to enhance creativity are discussed in Chapter 4, the text not only addresses college papers and projects, but it also explains the ways in which enhanced creativity can solve problems at work or a different perspective may help to resolve a difficult personal problem. When time management is discussed in Chapter 7, the text not only explains its strategies in the context of college courses, but it also points out that when time is well managed, one has more time (or at least some time if one is a busy student) to pursue enjoyable personal activities. *The Master Student Guide* also advises that it is essential to make some time for these personal activities in order to relieve stress, ensure one's emotional well-being, and, ultimately, achieve academic or professional success.

By working to develop those areas that will help students to achieve academic success, but also by using a whole-life context in which to address a student's college career, it is hoped that students will be able to more fully relate and appreciate the purpose, strategies, and lessons developed in *The Master Student Guide to Academic Success*. It is often a struggle to ensure that students use the books they purchase. We believe that the academic/whole-life conceptualization of the *Guide*; its unique structure as reference guide and/or textbook; its distinctive use of tabs, checklists, sidebars, and the like; and its consequent utility will make it both desirable for students and attractive to instructors. Ultimately, we believe that the more useful the *Guide* is, the more likely a student will be to use it.

In addition to the teaching strategies and resources for readings found in this manual, be sure to visit the accompanying Instructor's website for additional support. You can access the quizzes, exercises, and sample syllabi and customize them for your course. Additional resources are also available. Visit the site at http://masterstudent.college.hmco.com/instructors.

Features of the Text

Tabs

One of the most significant features of this text is the tabbed section markers. Not only do these tabs provide a tactile aid in easily navigating through the text's twenty-nine chapters, but they also provide a detailed breakdown of each chapter, including page references for all major subtopics. Using the bulleted chapter summaries provided on the tabbed pages, students can get a quick breakdown of all the major strategies related to any topic—for instance, steps to choosing a major, ways to use the Cornell Format method, tips to creating an outline, plans for presentations, or problem-solving procedures.

Checklists, Examples, and Sidebars

Throughout the text are checklists, examples, and sidebars that help students further connect with the concepts presented. These features range from sample research paper outlines to sidebars on tips for balancing your time to checklists for four-year career planning. These features provide a powerful statement on how the strategies and concepts in the text can be practically applied to daily life.

Ways to Experiment with Strategies in the Chapter

The final section of Chapter 2 introduces an exercise that is unique to the *Master Student Guide to Academic Success* and can be an extremely effective tool to reinforce and strengthen the learning that has taken place previously within the chapter. The section titled "Experiment with Learning Strategies" concludes Chapter 2 and each of the following chapters found in the *Guide.* These "Experiments" are designed to help students test the suggestions and information presented in the preceding sections of each chapter and change their behavior over the long term. The steps in these exercises are based on the subject matter that is explained in each chapter.

In this "Experiment with Learning Strategies" section, students will be asked to quickly review the information and suggestions presented in the chapter (which can be done easily by referring to the tabbed section at the front of the chapter). Students should then pick a suggestion or skill to implement. They will practice and incorporate this behavior and skill into their lives over the next week, at which point they will evaluate how well the suggestion worked for them. If it worked well, they should consider adopting it permanently and making it a habit. If not, they should try another suggestion in order to find what works best for them and to develop a series of academic and life skills that will enhance their achievement and success.

As an instructor, you should reinforce the "Experiment with Learning Strategies" and ensure that students actively perform and complete them. You should require that students report their results back to you in some way, for example, through a journal, short report format, class discussion, or brief presentation. The greatest benefit is gained from these exercises when students participate in them actively and seriously in order to develop a portfolio of effective skills that can be used whenever needed so they can enhance their academic success. It is your responsibility to help make sure that this happens.

Overview of Text

There are many different types of professors and instructors. With this comes different teaching methodologies, ways to set up and structure a course, and avenues and methods by which to deliver course content and knowledge. And, of course, students are diverse in their learning styles. One of the greatest strengths of the *Master Student Guide to Academic Success* is its flexibility. The text itself can serve many different purposes: as a main textbook, as an ancillary resource, as a reference guide with no main text required, or as a suggested reference guide.

As a Textbook

The *Master Student Guide to Academic Success* is comprehensive in its selection of the topics that students need to master in order to achieve academic success. It is well suited for use as a primary textbook in a traditional College Survival, Student Success, or first-year course. All necessary topics, including chapters on the cycle of learning (Chapter 1), creativity (Chapter 4), and research (Chapters 20 and 21), provide the professor with ample material for a traditional credit-bearing, textbook-driven college course. The *Master Student Guide*, along with this Instructor's Resource Manual, provide extensive lecture material, topics for discussion, exercises, activities, quizzes, and references for additional material that can be used to expand and supplement each chapter.

As a Supplemental Text

The role of the *Master Student Guide* is not limited to that of main textbook. Given its unique format and structure, it is also ideal for use in other ways, such as an ancillary guide to a main textbook. Chapters and topics, as well as exercises and activities, can be assigned selectively and independently to supplement another textbook that is used as the primary vehicle for classroom lecture and course structure. Meanwhile, the *Master Student Guide* is still available for the student to use as a resource if she needs help in an area that might not be covered by other lecture material or course work, such as Making Effective Presentations (Chapter 25). The *Guide's* easy-to-use structure and accessible style and tone, especially with the tabbed format, make it an attractive resource guide for students to use to supplement individual weaknesses or gaps in their skill levels.

As a Resource Guide

In still other instances, some instructors prefer to teach a College Success or First Year Seminar course without a textbook. Given the nature of the subject matter, the use of the course as a bonding experience for students, a focus on building student self-confidence and self-esteem, and even the use of the course as a retention tool, some professors choose to structure their courses on their own and develop campus specific content. It is often difficult to find a single textbook that encompasses these diverse areas in a single title, thereby providing further incentive for an instructor to teach such a course without a primary text. In these cases, the *Master Student Guide* can serve as a useful and powerful resource guide to support the professor's individually created and textbook-free curriculum. Individual topics, chapters, and activities can be identified easily and assigned separately to supplement the instructor's own lessons when needed. Or the *Guide* can provide individualized support for a single student or a group of students whom the instructor has identified as deficient in some area or who themselves feel are insecure in a particular skill area.

As a Reference Guide

In addition, the *Master Student Guide* may be used by a professor simply as a suggested independent reference guide. The book's many essential and easily found topics within its well-organized and tabbed structure make it an excellent source of support for a student to have available when he encounters academic problems or difficulty. Although a professor may choose neither to lecture directly from any of the chapters nor to formally assign any of the exercises or activities in the *Guide*, he can recommend the *Master Student Guide for Academic Success* to his students so they have a source of academic support readily available at all times. In this way, a student will always have easy access to note- and test-taking skills (Chapters 11–15, 18–19), time management techniques (Chapter 7), exercises for creativity enhancement (Chapter 4), ways to relieve math anxiety (Chapter 29), and many other topics that help to overcome obstacles to academic achievement.

So far, the *Master Student Guide* has been discussed as a tool in the teaching of a fairly traditional College Success or First-Year course. There is no doubt that this guide can serve as an excellent textbook or reference guide for a course of this type. The objective of such courses, as well as one of the primary objectives of this book, is to provide an orientation to college life and to provide the skills necessary to achieve academic success. Therefore, the *Master Student Guide* is entirely appropriate and highly recommended for these courses. However, its unique structure, independence of topics, tabbed format, and well-organized layout and design give this book great flexibility for use in many additional situations encountered in the world of higher education.

For Major-Specific Courses

The flexibility built into the *Guide* by giving students the ability to easily select independent topics for study makes this book an excellent choice for a reference guide as well as a textbook. This greatly expands the potential uses for this title. For example, the *Master Student Guide* could be used as a suggested or required reference guide for major-specific courses. In this context, it becomes an important source of information for students who discover personal deficiencies in some area that inhibit their performance in their course work at any time in their academic careers. An instructor in these courses would seldom take class time to address these individual challenges, and some students might be too intimidated to admit their frustration and deficiency and, therefore, not seek the help that they need. The *Master Student Guide* would be a valuable resource to guide students through these difficult academic areas. Any professor could feel confident that her students would be able to easily use this guide as a first resource to help them to overcome obstacles encountered in many of their courses.

For Learning Communities

In related circumstances, many courses are now linked together as part of learning communities. That is, for example, common themes or topics are taught across several courses to a common group of students in a given semester. Although these courses and "communities" are clearly designed to enhance the academic experience for students and promote educational success, there are some students who still might encounter difficulty in the classroom or with the material taught. Yet a support structure to deal with the deficiencies of individual students that are not easily apparent may not be readily accessible. Nor would the instructor necessarily be able to accommodate such deficiencies with increased classroom attention when so much course content must be covered. Here again, the *Master Student Guide* makes an excellent resource to help students meet such challenges and avoid being left behind.

Learning communities, as described earlier, can be developed and used anywhere within a two- or four-year college curriculum, and the *Master Student Guide* is an appropriate resource tool to support learning at any time. However, often a group of courses within a student's first semester in the first year of college are grouped or linked together in order to provide an enriched learning experience, a supportive environment, and a situation in which the students have the opportunity to connect and establish meaningful relationships with each other. Some college programs do not offer or require a full College Success or First Year Experience course. And if such a course is offered at an institution, it is almost certainly included in this type of early learning community in order to help promote success. The *Master Student Guide* clearly becomes an important tool in either situation.

If a specific College Success course is not part of the learning community of classes, then the *Guide* becomes a principal source of reference for professors to use and recommend to students in situations in which they need additional help and guidance during their first year. If an actual College Success or Survival course is part of the learning community, then the *Master Student Guide* becomes an integral part of the curriculum. The text is written across the curriculum, including sections on research (Chapters 21–22), presentations and public speaking (Chapter 25), organization (Chapter 7), generating ideas (Chapter 4), decision-making and problem-solving (Chapter 5), math anxiety (Chapter 29), and many others. Obviously, just as academic content is taught across classes in these learning communities, so too these skills are important across the linked curriculum. The *Guide* offers an accessible, easy-to-teach, and easy-to-use tool for instructors in both the First Year Seminar class and the other academic courses within the learning community. The *Guide* allows the skill and support topics described within to be easily connected to the academic content in each of the linked courses. It fits neatly into the purpose of the learning community: to enhance and increase academic success through a focused and linked approach.

For Orientation Programs

The classroom structures described previously can be characterized as the more traditional, full course-length (or nearly so) types, including those within the learning communities. By this time, it is clear how the *Master Student Guide to Academic Success* can very effectively serve as a textbook within these courses or as a primary reference guide supporting them. However, there are many other less traditional first- year and academic support structures in which the *Guide* can serve an equally important and effective purpose. Some colleges do not offer their College Success course as a full semester-length course, but instead utilize another structure, such as a summer orientation session or a brief (three- to eight-week) first-year orientation program within the student's first semester or term. Due to the ease with which topics, activities, and exercises can be found (using the tabbed format), selected, rearranged, and skipped over, the *Master Student Guide* is an excellent resource for these programs in which a select amount of focused material needs to be covered. At the same time, the student has a text to take with him for his own use and review that clearly explains the topics that could not be covered within the program. And, of course, the *Guide* serves as a reference book for use whenever a student needs additional help or encounters a new academic problem.

For Workshops

Some colleges and universities continue to provide support for their students beyond their first-year experience and throughout their academic careers. They often do this through workshops targeted to specific student–centered areas, such as career development, test-taking strategies, resumé writing, creative thinking, leadership, and many others. The *Master Student Guide* can support many of these workshops as well by providing an excellent source of easy-to-find information. In addition, the text provides several activities for each topic that would be appropriate for use in a workshop setting. Furthermore, upon completion of the workshop the participant has a guide to take with him for review of the material that was covered, for future reference of all included topics (which can contribute to academic, personal, and professional success), or for use at future workshops. Perhaps an entire series of workshops could even be developed around The *Master Student Guide to Academic Success*. Students could participate in those workshops that cover topics of interest to them or in which they feel they need a quick refresher and at the same time take away a reference guide that allows for additional independent review and help on topics that might be needed in the future but were not covered at the workshop that they attended.

For Online Courses

The *Guide*'s easy-to-use structure and accessible style also make it a good fit for an online course structure, where more intimate student/instructor contact is less frequent, or not present at all. With minimal guidance, students are able to find the information they need on the vast range of topics present in the text. For additional support specifically in the area of online learning, the *Guide* is easily paired with *E-Learning Companion* by Ryan Watkins and Michael Corry (Houghton Mifflin Company, ©2005). Ask your sales rep about packaging these texts together for your course.

For Nontraditional Students

Finally, we have not yet specifically addressed the subject of the nontraditional adult learner who makes up an increasing percentage of college students. This segment of the college population is diverse, often attends college part-time, is usually employed either full- or part-time, may have increased family responsibilities including children to care for, and includes students at different levels of academic preparation. Two characteristics are clear: the adult learner has many responsibilities, and he has been away from the classroom and the world of education for some length of time, from a few years up to several decades. These students have different needs than those of traditional, eighteen-year-old first-year students.

At the same time, colleges and universities do not always provide these students with the same type of first-year support that they do traditional students. Nontraditional students often attend college part-time or in evening or weekend programs. Given their personal and professional responsibilities, they often attend accelerated programs. It is often believed that the lives and schedules of these students leaves little room to accommodate traditional College Survival programs. As a result, topics that are often essential for academic support and success are left to an orientation evening, voluntary workshops, or worst of all, never offered to the adult learner. Yet, in many ways, this group of students faces the highest risk of not achieving its academic goals.

The *Master Student Guide to Academic Success* is an obvious resource for the adult learner. First, it includes the nontraditional student in its audience. It addresses the challenges, responsibilities, and demands placed on their lives. It incorporates the need for all students to balance many different aspects of their lives while focusing on the achievement of academic success. It references specific examples of situations faced by the nontraditional adult learner, thereby allowing him to identify with the challenges faced by those pursuing higher education. It clearly and specifically includes the adult learner and works to make her a part of the education process by referencing and representing her unique responsibilities and challenges. And it offers specific suggestions and strategies for overcoming her particular obstacles and achieving academic success.

Second, the *Master Student Guide* is an excellent textbook or resource guide for an orientation program, First-Year Experience (FYE) workshop, or College Survival seminar. Unfortunately, the adult learner will most likely experience his College Success studies in this format instead of a semester-long, traditionally structured FYE course. The format of the *Guide* allows for its easy adaptation to this purpose. The professor conducting the seminar chooses only the chapters and activities that specifically support the material that he covers in the seminar. Meanwhile, the student has a resource to take with her from the seminar that can be used to reference any topics that she needs that were not covered in the orientation seminar and to use to support her learning throughout her college career.

Finally, in cases where no College Success or FYE seminar of any kind are offered for the nontraditional learner, students can use the *Master Student Guide* as a comprehensive reference guide to support their academic studies. The *Guide* is structured and organized for quick and easy reference. It is comprehensive and includes all areas that will affect a student's academic success. It is clearly written, easy to understand, and also easy to use independently in order to manage time efficiently, balance conflicting responsibilities, develop the skills needed to achieve academic success, and continue on to a satisfying career after college.

Creating Your Syllabus

When the *Master Student Guide to Academic Success* was written, the order of the chapters and the topics covered therein were carefully developed with two objectives in mind. First, if used in its complete and ordered format, the book could fully accommodate a student's transition into the world of higher education and beyond. Second, and perhaps more importantly, the chapters are organized, tabbed for ease of reference, and structured so that each one can be used independently of the others or in small groups of short chapters that completely address a subject area. The structure of the chapters allows each to stand on its own, providing the instructor with the flexibility to reorganize the curriculum to the unique needs of his particular teaching situation. This gives the *Guide* the added ability to be used effectively in a variety of situations outside of the traditional First-Year Experience course (see the Overview of Text section earlier for a description of possible course types).

One of the goals of the *Master Student Guide* is to be comprehensive in its coverage of the skills needed by students to be successful in their academic pursuits. It accomplishes this goal by grouping twenty-nine chapters into seven sections: Making Successful Transitions (Chapters 1 and 2); Thinking Critically and Creatively (Chapters 3–5); Planning to Succeed (Chapters 6–8); Reading and Note-Taking with a Purpose (Chapters 9–15); Building Memory and Test Skills (Chapters 16–19); Developing and Presenting Ideas (Chapters 20–27); and Succeeding in Math and Science (Chapters 28 and 29). Therefore, the *Master Student Guide* can easily be used in its present format and order in a traditional semester-long College Success or First-Year Experience course. In contrast, you do not have to cover everything in the book, and you do not have to maintain the order suggested in the table of contents. For example, you may prefer to introduce the study skills sections much earlier or to skip one or more chapters. Each chapter is clearly tabbed, including a Quick Reference Guide on the tab itself, which makes finding information and the rearrangement of topics easy and convenient. Since every college and class is different, you may want to choose among the topics covered and customize your course to fit your students' needs. One of the *Guide*'s great strengths is that it allows you to do so.

To these ends, the *Guide* first addresses and introduces the world of higher education and advanced learning to the student. It sets the context in which the student will be participating and learning, including those nonacademic elements that a student might encounter and that could influence and impact her learning environment and success (Chapters 1 and 2). The purpose is to make the student feel comfortable in his strange new surroundings and to understand that it is normal to come upon obstacles and maybe even feel out of place or overwhelmed at times.

In the next two sections, the *Guide* addresses creativity and problem solving (Chapters 3–5), followed by goal setting (Chapters 6–8). Goal setting is first discussed in the broadest terms for the student, that of life purpose and career goals. Such broad life goals are often difficult to identify clearly; therefore, the chapters on creativity and decision-making are included first. Strategies and skills to enhance creativity, develop ideas, and improve decision making and problem solving are included in these chapters. Therefore, students will be fully equipped to undertake the large issues of identifying a life purpose and setting goals that follow in the next section. When life and career goals are clearly identified and clarified, they can give important meaning to a student's studies and course work. It is for this reason that the chapter on goal setting is structured in this way, from the initial identification of the broadest goals down to the establishment of smaller weekly or daily goals.

Once the context of the academic environment is laid out in these first eight chapters, the clear academic skills are each examined in turn. The next twenty-one chapters are grouped into four specific sections that address the following subject areas: reading and note-taking; memory and test-taking skills; developing and presenting ideas (which includes research, draft writing, and revision, among others); and succeeding in math and science. A course syllabus can easily be constructed that follows this order of chapters. (See below for a sample.) Or you could easily customize the order of chapters to your individual course requirements (see p. 11 for a sample of such a customized syllabus) for use in a three-, two-, or even one-credit course.

In addition to its traditional uses, the *Master Student Guide* is also intended to be used in many nontraditional formats, such as learning communities, workshops, orientations, and many others. In order to accomplish this, the *Guide* is clearly tabbed so that topics can be found quickly and information referenced easily. Chapters are written and topics are developed so they can stand alone. This allows the professor or instructor to adapt the order in which they are taught to the unique needs of his particular teaching situation. This flexibility and organization also allows the instructor to select only those chapters that support individual topics in a variety of possible teaching formats, while allowing the students to use the rest of the *Guide* as a reference book when needed in any of their courses.

Several sample syllabi are given. The first (Syllabus A) will follow the chapters as ordered in the *Master Student Guide* in a traditional semester-length College Success or First-Experience course. The next syllabus (Syllabus B) provides an example of a course structure wherein the instructor has manipulated the order in which chapters are covered for his own customized purpose. The final syllabus (Syllabus C) will illustrate the *Guide's* use in a less traditional format, where certain chapters will be chosen to support specific lessons or purposes and other chapters will not be covered at all in the classroom, but will be left for students to review independently or to be used as academic reference when needed. This sample syllabus will be more like a lesson outline or seminar agenda than a traditional course syllabus.

Please feel free to use the *Master Student Guide* in the way that best supports your teaching objectives. One of the *Guide's* great strengths is its flexibility. Take advantage of the fact that it can be adapted easily to fit your particular teaching situation.

Sample Syllabus A
The First-Year Experience

Course Purpose: This course is designed to help you succeed in college and in life. In it, you will learn many proven strategies for creating greater academic, professional, and personal success. This course is a learning opportunity that will orient and guide you through the first semester of your college experience. In addition, it will teach and provide you with many of the skills and strategies that will enable you to achieve success throughout your college life and will remain important long after graduation day.

Course Objectives: In this course, you will learn to:
Maximize your learning. You will discover the natural process of effective learning and understand how to apply that process to your individual learning style preference. This knowledge will enable you to earn better grades in college and also to be a more effective lifelong learner.
Improve creative and critical thinking skills. You will learn how to develop and enhance the thinking skills and processes that are essential for making decisions and solving problems in your academic, professional, and personal lives.
Master effective study skills. You will learn how to improve essential skills such as reading, note-taking, memorization, studying, and test-taking.

Write more effectively. You will learn how to improve your writing skills by learning effective writing and research strategies, utilizing writing practices, and writing essays and journal entries. *Raise your self-esteem.* You will learn how to develop self-acceptance, self-respect, and self-confidence.

Course Supplies:

1. *Master Student Guide to Academic Success*, Doug Toft, editor
2. Journal

Grading:

Quizzes	50 points
Autobiography	50 points
Presentations (2)	50 points
Journal Entries	50 points
Group projects (5)	100 points
Attendance/Participation	100 points
Total Possible Points	400

Schedule

Week #1	Introduction	
	Chapter 1	Entering the Culture of Higher Education
	Chapter 2	Using the Cycle of Learning
Week #2	Chapter 2	Using the Cycle of Learning
	Chapter 3	Evaluating Ideas
Week #3	Chapter 4	Creating New Ideas
	Chapter 5	Making Decisions and Solving Problems
Week #4	Chapter 6	Choosing Your Life Purpose and Goals
Week #5	Chapter 7	Managing Your Time
Week #6	Chapter 8	Choosing Your Major and Planning Your Career
Week #7	Chapter 9	Using Three Steps to Active Reading
	Chapter 10	Becoming a Flexible Reader
Week #8	Chapter 11	Using Seven Tools for Powerful Notes
	Chapter 12	Notes: Experimenting with the Cornell Format
Week #9	Chapter 13	Notes: Experimenting with Maps
	Chapter 14	Notes: Experimenting with Outlines
	Chapter 15	Creating More Value from Your Notes
Week #10	Chapter 16	Memory: Storing Ideas and Information
	Chapter 17	Memory: Recalling Ideas and Information
Week #11	Chapter 18	Preparing for Tests
	Chapter 19	Using Test Time Efficiently
Week #12	Chapter 20	Research: Defining What You Want to Discover
	Chapter 21	Research: Using Sources of Information
Week #13	Chapter 22	Preparing to Write
	Chapter 23	Writing a Draft
	Chapter 24	Revising a Draft
Week #14	Chapter 25	Making Effective Presentations
	Chapter 26	Using Computers to Promote Your Success
	Chapter 27	Becoming a Member of the Online Community
Week #15	Chapter 28	Mastering Math and Science
	Chapter 29	Reducing Math and Science Anxiety
		Wrap-Up

Sample Syllabus B
The First-Year Experience

Course Purpose: This course is designed to help you succeed in college and in life. In it you will learn many proven strategies for creating greater academic, professional, and personal success. This course is a learning opportunity that will orient and guide you through the first semester of your college experience. In addition, it will teach and provide you with many of the skills and strategies that will enable you to achieve success throughout your college life and will remain important long after graduation day.

Course Objectives: In this course, you will learn to:
Maximize your learning. You will discover the natural process of effective learning and understand how to apply that process to your individual learning style preference. This knowledge will enable you to earn better grades in college and also to be a more effective lifelong learner.
Improve creative and critical thinking skills. You will learn how to develop and enhance the thinking skills and processes that are essential for making decisions and solving problems in your academic, professional, and personal lives.
Master effective study skills. You will learn how to improve essential skills such as reading, note-taking, memorization, studying, and test-taking.
Write more effectively. You will learn how to improve your writing skills by learning effective writing and research strategies, utilizing writing practices, and writing essays and journal entries.
Raise your self-esteem. You will learn how to develop self-acceptance, self-respect, and self-confidence.

Course Supplies:

1. *Master Student Guide to Academic Success*, Doug Toft, editor
2. Journal

Grading:

Quizzes	50 points
Autobiography	50 points
Presentations (2)	50 points
Journal Entries	50 points
Group projects (5)	100 points
Attendance/Participation	100 points
Total Possible Points	400

Schedule

Week #1	Introduction	
	Chapter 1	Entering the Culture of Higher Education
	Chapter 2	Using the Cycle of Learning
Week #2	Chapter 3	Evaluating Ideas
	Chapter 4	Creating New Ideas
Week #3	Chapter 5	Making Decisions and Solving Problems
	Chapter 6	Choosing Your Life Purpose and Goals
Week #4	Chapter 6	Choosing Your Life Purpose and Goals
	Chapter 8	Choosing Your Major and Planning Your Career
Week #5	Chapter 7	Managing Your Time
Week #6	Chapter 28	Mastering Math and Science

	Chapter 29	Reducing Math and Science Anxiety
Week #7	Chapter 18	Preparing for Tests
	Chapter 19	Using Test Time Efficiently
	Chapter 25	Making Effective Presentations
Week #8	Chapter 25	Making Effective Presentations
	Chapter 9	Using Three Steps to Active Reading
	Chapter 10	Becoming a Flexible Reader
Week #9	Chapter 11	Using Seven Tools for Powerful Notes
	Chapter 12	Notes: Experimenting with the Cornell Format
Week #10	Chapter 13	Notes: Experimenting with Maps
	Chapter 14	Notes: Experimenting with Outlines
	Chapter 15	Creating More Value from Your Notes
Week #11	Chapter 16	Memory: Storing Ideas and Information
	Chapter 17	Memory: Recalling Ideas and Information
Week #12	Chapter 20	Research: Defining What You Want to Discover
	Chapter 21	Research: Using Sources of Information
Week #13	Chapter 22	Preparing to Write
	Chapter 23	Writing a Draft
Week #14	Chapter 23	Writing a Draft
	Chapter 24	Revising a Draft
Week #15	Chapter 26	Using Computers to Promote Your Success
	Chapter 27	Becoming a Member of the Online Community
		Wrap-Up

Sample Syllabus C
Outline in Support of a Core Course, Orientation, or Some Other Specific Purpose

Purpose: This outline is designed to cover selected topics that will help a student to achieve success in the academic course that it supports or the learning community or purpose to which it is linked.

		Possible Topics
Lesson #1	Chapter 1	Entering the Culture of Higher Education
Lesson #2	Chapter 4	Creating New Ideas
	Chapter 5	Making Decisions and Solving Problems
Lesson #3	Chapter 6	Choosing Your Life Purpose and Goals
	Chapter 7	Managing Your Time
Lesson #4	Chapter 9	Using Three Steps to Active Reading
Lesson #5	Chapter 11	Using Seven Tools to Powerful Notes
	Chapter 15	Creating More Value from Your Notes
Lesson #6	Chapter18	Preparing for Tests
	Chapter 19	Using Test Time Efficiently
Lesson #7	Chapter 22	Preparing to Write
	Chapter 23	Writing a Draft
	Chapter 24	Revising Your Draft
Lesson #8	Chapter 25	Making Effective Presentations
	Chapter 26	Using Computers to Promote Your Success
	Chapter 27	Becoming a Member of the Online Community

Chapter-by-Chapter Resources

Overview of Chapter Resources

In the pages that follow, each chapter of the *Master Student Guide* is discussed and strategies for presenting key concepts to your students are given. These strategies include lecture ideas, classroom discussion topics, and exercises and activities. Because the Guide is flexible and designed to fit with almost any course structure or student population, care has been taken to allow these tips and strategies to accommodate a broad range of scenarios. In many instances, suggestions are given for adapting strategies and activities to specific situations or recommendations are made for where they may be most appropriate. However, because you as the instructor know your course the best, you may find it necessary to adapt these strategies on your own to provide the most benefit to your students.

Many of the concepts that students learn in their first-year experience (FYE) course require hands-on use in order to gain maximum benefit. Consequently, many of the strategies presented in the following pages involve ways to get your students to practice what they have learned in the *Master Student Guide*. The "Additional Activities and Exercises" at the end of each chapter discussion that follows offer many ways for your students to manipulate and work with concepts and strategies. Many of these activities involve group discussion and projects in which students literally perform suggestions from the text either for courses they are currently taking or for scenarios that you as the instructor require for the course. If a particular format does not fit with your particular course structure—for instance, group exercises may not be feasible for commuter campuses or online courses—you may need to adapt the specifications.

Additionally, because they do not present a quantifiable "right" or "wrong" answer, these group activities and discussions may be difficult to align with your grading structure. In this case, I suggest requiring students to complete a journal or summary essay at the conclusion of the class period, in which they describe their impressions or cite examples of strategies that they have learned. You may need to be creative in designing requirements for these entries: ask students to list three key points of the discussion, have students choose a strategy that they will commit to employing over the coming week, and then follow up with them on this.

Grading in many of these activities will have to be subjective and based on participation. One suggestion is to plan the total number of activities that will be used throughout the course, and give students credit for each exercise in which they participated or they successfully completed. The work would not be evaluated for a grade; credit would be given solely on participation.

Another similar method for grading would be to plan out all of the activities but weigh appropriate exercises according to the quality of their work or completeness. A scale could be created using several levels. For example, participating and completing work of minimum quality would receive only partial credit, where work of superior quality would receive full credit.

Another interesting variation is to allow students to evaluate the work of their classmates, and include this feedback as part of the activity grade. Obviously, this suggestion would be more complex to execute, but it might be a good way to more meaningfully include these exercises in the student's grade.

Making Successful Transitions

Chapter 1: Entering the Culture of Higher Education

Change is difficult; sometimes it can even be frightening. Most people are not comfortable when they do not know what the results of their actions will be. Most people do not like the unfamiliar or unknown. Since change involves moving into the unknown, it can bring feelings of discomfort, stress, and anxiety. As discussed at the beginning of the manual, college is a time of transition for all students, and they will be faced with drastic changes in their lives, no matter what their backgrounds or stations in life.

Even a young first-year student who lives at home, has been successful academically, and begins her college career directly upon completing high school might find her new environment different than what she has previously known. The level of work might be higher than she previously experienced, the volume of work might be greater than before, professors might be less accessible and less available than high school teachers, more independence and individual decision-making might be required of her, and more responsibility for her own studies and actions will probably be required. The same is true for the student who has been in the workforce and is now stepping in to the classroom for the first time in many years. If a student does not manage this transition well, he is not likely to achieve a high level of academic success. In the worst case, he might even decide not to return for his second semester.

As an instructor during a student's first year or, more importantly, during his first semester, you have two important goals beyond providing knowledge in your subject area. First, you want each student to recognize and understand that all of the feelings just described are natural and shared by other students to some degree. Some amount of anxiety is normal and should be expected. It should be acknowledged, accepted, and turned into positive action.

Second, you want to transform the unfamiliar into the familiar. In order to do this, you need to provide information to your students. The more information that you can give to your students and the earlier in the semester you can get it to them, the more comfortable they will be in their new surroundings and the more likely they will be able to successfully manage change.

This chapter will help students:

- acknowledge and confront change in a new and unfamiliar environment.
- accept feelings of moderate uncertainty, stress, or anxiety.
- focus on the positive, develop a positive attitude.
- understand the differences between high school and higher education.
- find support services and systems.
- get involved in organizations and events.
- understand diversity.
- understand the importance of financial planning and responsibility.
- understand the relationship of good health to academic success.

Suggestions for Teaching

As an instructor who will help to introduce your students to the culture of higher education and help them to adapt to and deal with change in their lives, you should work to make your students feel knowledgeable about and comfortable in their new environment. You should also try to help them to understand change and uncertainty and to feel comfortable dealing with it. The best way to begin to achieve these ends is to provide your students with information. In the initial days of class, you should provide your students with information about the college or school, the campus, their program(s)/major(s), support services available to them both on campus and in the local community, and campus activities.

In addition, you should provide information about your FYE or College Success course, including your goals and expectations for your students. You should also consider discussing the content and expectations of courses in which your students are likely to be enrolled in their first semester or common courses that have previously been selected for enrollment by this group of students (such as those linked in a learning community).

However, keep in mind that you do not want to overwhelm students by presenting too much too quickly. The goal is not to present as much information as possible in the shortest amount of time, but to present the most useful information that your students are most likely to need. Choose carefully, considering value not volume. Given these considerations, there will still be a large amount of material to present. If you are including this chapter as part of a College Survival course, consider delivering your information over several class sessions. Remember that your students' level of comfort with their new environment and also with your class will be greater if they feel that you are genuinely interested in their well-being and success, not simply rushing to cover too much material in too short a time.

If possible, take your students on a tour, even if it is only a tour of your building or the library. A trip outside of the classroom is usually a positive experience, and it conveys your willingness to go beyond the minimum expectations that an instructor provides information. Invite guest speakers to come in to talk about their areas of expertise or responsibility. Utilize staff members from Financial Services, the Library, Academic Affairs, and Student Services. It is beneficial for students to be able to associate a face with a name or a department. You may want to invite a wide variety of speakers and spread out their visits over several weeks, thereby adding diversity to the structure of your course. Look for the best speakers that you can find in each department, that is, those who present their information in a way that is interesting and exciting to your students.

Another possible lesson is a discussion of the differences between high school and college life or, for nontraditional adult learners, the differences in their lives before and after enrolling in college. Actively solicit the opinions and views of your students here so that you can direct the lecture to some of their specific concerns. This lesson can be used as an opportunity to provide more general information about the college experience, assess the expectations of your students, reinforce those that are accurate, and correct those that are not.

Finally, as pointed out earlier, one of the goals of this chapter is to make your students feel comfortable with their new environment and with transition and change. You should also try to make them feel comfortable asking for help when they encounter a problem or a difficult situation. It is often difficult for people to admit that they are confused, overwhelmed, or do not know the answer. Students are no different. It is often intimidating for many students to talk to their professors when they are confused, falling behind, or not doing well in their courses. It is often difficult to seek out a stranger in the Student Services, Academic Affairs, or Financial Services departments and ask for help. You should help your students to understand that these feelings of confusion and anxiety are normal and that any embarrassment or intimidation in these situations is often felt by other students as well. These feelings should be confronted and overcome. What is most important is to ask for and to get help if they need it, so they can achieve the success that they desire.

Additional Activities and Exercises

Scavenger Hunt Divide the students in your class into groups. Create a scavenger hunt in which the groups must collect college facts or administrator names from key locations throughout the campus.

For example, have them collect the name of the library or the gymnasium, the name of the largest dormitory on campus, the name of the building in which the infirmary is located, and so on. Or have them collect the names of the academic provost, dean of the College of Liberal Arts, vice president of student affairs, and the like. A variation of this activity also could be conducted on line or using the college catalog.

Autobiography Have your students write a one-page autobiography. Consider having them focus on the key events in their lives that caused or influenced them to enroll in this particular college and program. You will be surprised by how much they want to tell you about themselves. This can be an excellent method to better understand your students, their goals, and the reasons why they enrolled in college.

Tour Take your students on a tour of important places on the college campus. You can also create a handout of the names of important places, administrators, and information and hand this out for reference at the beginning of the tour.

Credit Card Dangers Invite a financial planner to your class to discuss the potential dangers of credit card debt. (Also consider showing the video, "Money and Finances." See "Support and Resources" for more information on this video.)

First-Semester Journal Have students keep a journal that records their thoughts, feelings, and reactions to their first semester of college. These entries can help students to be more aware of the changes they are going through and give them a better perspective on their personal goals. Include this work in the grading requirements for the course in some way. You can periodically check the journal by sight to ensure that students are making regular entries, have students hand them in several times during the term for your review, or give students the option of either method.

Support Group Have each student develop a support group. Each student should identify and list people he or she can ask for help when confronted with particular obstacles, difficulties, or distractions. The list could include the names of, contact information for, and appropriate situations in which to call tutors, professors, other students, parents, fraternity brothers/sorority sisters, resident assistants, employers, and the like.

Chapter 2: Using the Cycle of Learning

As skilled instructors, we are intimately aware of the fact that not all students learn in the same ways. Many excellent theories, such as Gagne's Conditions of Learning, Social Learning Theory, Multiple Intelligences, Experiential Learning Theory, and many others, help us to understand the different ways in which our students learn. As a result of our realization that multiple learning styles are being employed by the students in each classroom, we are able employ a variety of teaching methodologies in order to reach the greatest number of students.

It is important as well for students to understand that there is more than one way to *perceive* and then *process* information. As developed and explained in the previous chapter, it is important to open students up to the challenges and potential benefits of learning at the collegiate level, not to shut them down. Toward that end, this chapter explains that it is normal and acceptable to learn differently; to need different things from course work, lectures, and professors; and to possess different skills. Sometimes a student's preferred learning style does not coincide with her professor's preferred teaching style, possibly resulting in frustration and academic performance below her normal expectations. This situation is not an impossible barrier to overcome but rather a temporary obstacle that requires the development of new or different strategies with which to work. Further, some students might feel that they are deficient in certain academic skill areas, that they don't know how to learn, or that they are not "good" at school. In reality, they need to determine how they best process information and work to adapt what is happening in the classroom to their particular styles and strengths.

This chapter will

- introduce the concept of learning styles.
- introduce and explain Kolb's Theory of Experiential Learning.
- help students to understand Kolb's four modes of learning.
- give examples of ways to use each of Kolb's four modes.
- allow students to explore and assess their learning styles in the context of Kolb's theory.
- help students to build the cycle of learning into their courses.
- address students' acceptance of change, discomfort, and the unknown in order to stretch and expand their knowledge so they can become better students.
- instruct students to take charge of their learning.
- explain diversity in relation to ethnicity, beliefs, and learning styles.
- offer ways to accommodate diverse or different learning styles in other students and thereby resolve conflicts between styles.

Suggestions for Teaching

Chapter 2 discusses learning theories and styles. Many students may not be familiar with the concept of different learning styles and the need to employ multiple learning methodologies in order to accommodate these different styles. Therefore, a brief discussion of these learning theories and teaching methods would provide an excellent introductory lesson for this chapter. Within this lesson, it also would be beneficial to remind students that no particular learning style is wrong or bad. They are simply different. The most important thing for a student to do is to identify his predominant learning style (be sure to use the exercises provided in the chapter for this purpose), so that he or she can use his or her strongest appropriate skill set as often as possible and be able to accommodate other styles when necessary.

Chapter 2 focuses on David Kolb's Theory of Experiential Learning. Kolb's theory identifies four modes in which learning takes place: concrete experience, reflective observation, abstract conceptualization, and active experimentation. Kolb's work can serve as a useful example of a *specific* theory of multiple learning styles, which can build upon the general concepts that you have previously discussed.

One of the most important goals of this chapter should be your students' identification of their own particular learning styles. You can use your preferred theory of learning styles or use Kolb's Theory of Experiential Learning, which is supported by explanations and exercises within the text. *The Master Student Guide to Academic Success* strongly advocates a hands-on approach to learning. Although a lecture format can be an excellent way to quickly provide useful information, we believe that the best way for new students to develop the important skills that will make them successful in their course work throughout their college careers is through performance and practice. Therefore, your students should perform some exercise in which they actively identify their preferred learning styles. An excellent and easily used checklist (for Kolb's framework) is provided for this purpose on page 24.

In addition, I recommend that whichever exercise you use for this purpose, you should have your students complete it as a classroom lesson. It is important that students take it seriously and spend a proper amount of time evaluating their styles. You will be able to stress the importance of the lesson and guide them through the evaluation process if it is performed in class rather than as a homework assignment. Upon completion of the guided self-evaluation, you can conduct another classroom discussion, encouraging your students to share their results with the class, say how they feel about their preferred learning style, and talk about whether they were surprised by the results. As a conclusion to this lesson, you can stress the importance of the completed exercise and how this knowledge can now benefit them as they approach all of their course work. Remind your students that this is not just an exercise that is now put aside but is in fact important knowledge and self-awareness upon which to build strategies that will help them to achieve academic success.

Note that Chapter 2 also provides an excellent sidebar (on page 26) that gives examples of ways to use each of Kolb's four modes of learning. This can provide a useful topic for student discussion, and you can even extend the concept by asking students to provide specific examples of each mode in their recent learning experiences.

Another important topic that you can use for discussion is the fact that professors also have different teaching styles and methods. In some situations a professor's favored teaching method may not be the most appropriate style to accommodate a student's best learning style. Every student will certainly encounter this dilemma at some point in her college course work. So what does a student do when this happens? Accept the situation and make the best of a bad match? Or build on the identification and awareness of learning styles developed in the previous lessons? As previously stated, the *Master Student Guide* advocates that students take control and responsibility of their education. Therefore, this discussion can focus students on positive ways to accept and accommodate those teaching methods that might be at odds with their learning styles. They should not give up and accept a lower grade. They should not become frustrated, negative, and disruptive. You can counsel your students on the value of developing positive and open communications with their instructors. You can encourage them to speak with an instructor to explain the difficulty they may be having. It is also probably wise to remind your students that a few instructors may not always be receptive to discussion, communication, and disagreement. Outline strategies to modify your students' learning styles and to rely on less preferred, but still effective, styles and behaviors to accommodate this less than ideal relationship. This is a valuable lesson from which many students could benefit, since many students are often reluctant to share their feelings with a professor, ask for help, or confess that they are having difficulty. And in the worst case, there are some students who become frustrated and negative.

You may want to expand your discussion to include the different learning styles of other people whom students encounter when working on group projects in school or on the job. Here the focus is not on oneself, but on how others learn and, consequently, act and behave--and how the actions of these other people affect your performance. This topic is often overlooked, but it is still particularly important since students will find themselves in these situations throughout their years in school and thereafter in the workplace. Your lessons here will help your students to develop strategies to adjust their styles, to accommodate themselves to the styles of others, and to take advantage of the strengths of others to build synergy within a group.

Additional Activities and Exercises

Learning Style Assessment Have students identify their preferred learning styles according to David Kolb's Theory of Experiential Learning. Use the checklist "Explore Your Learning Styles" on page 24 of the *Master Student Guide to Academic Success*.

Learning Situations Have each student identify a learning situation in which he or she has participated during the previous week. Have them write a brief description of this situation and then answer the following questions. How was the information presented? Which of Kolb's four modes of learning would be most appropriate to use in the situation? Why? Is this your preferred learning style?

If not, can you approach the material or situation in a different way so that you can use your preferred style? Upon completing this exercise, students could then discuss the learning situations that they have chosen and their feelings about them. Discussing learning styles with each other will allow your students to see the variations and how they affect other people's perceptions and information processing. It will also provide an opportunity for students to pick up tips and strategies from one another, or even to locate possible future study partners—both those who share their style as well as those who don't.

Teaching Methods Have each member of the class give one (different) teaching strategy that would benefit them in the classroom. Use these suggestions to create a list of suggested or preferred teaching methods.

Discomfort Solutions Split your students into several groups. Have each group list all of the things that make them uncomfortable in the classroom and that they do not like about the learning/teaching process. Give out a prize to the group that creates the largest list in a limited time period. Have each group go back to its list and propose a way to remove the discomfort or positively change the teaching process in each of the items that they listed. Have each group present its solutions to the class. Give out a prize to each group that solves every item on its list.

Four Modes Have each student list Kolb's four modes of learning on a piece of paper. Beneath each heading, each student should list ways that he or she can use each mode.
As an extension of this exercise, have each student use each mode of learning in one of the ways that he or she has listed in an actual academic situation. Have them record and analyze each mode's use, its results, and their feelings about it (whether it was effective, easy or difficult to use, etc.).

Learning Journal Keep a journal for two weeks or more. In the journal, each student should briefly review how information is presented in each session of each of his or her classes during the designated period. Students should identify which of Kolb's four modes of learning they actually used in each class session. Was this a preferred method of learning? If not, why was it used? What accommodations were made to learn by this method?

Responsibility Conduct a discussion with your students where they develop and list all of the ways in which they can take responsibility for their education. Record their responses on the board. Transcribe the responses onto a single page, and distribute it to your students at their next class session.

Guest Speaker Invite a counselor or psychologist from your school to speak to the students about learning-style theories. This will give your students an opportunity to ask questions as well as become acquainted with a resource they can go to on their own.

Thinking Critically and Creatively

Chapter 3: Evaluating Ideas

Critical thinking requires the ability to evaluate ideas effectively. It underlies reading, speaking, listening, and writing. The ability to perform these four key tasks well, and to think critically, greatly increases a student's chances of achieving academic success. This is one of the major goals of a liberal education and an essential requirement in skill-driven classes such as engineering, biology, organic chemistry, marketing research, and the like.

This chapter, along with Chapters 4 (Creating New Ideas) and 5 (Making Decisions and Solving Problems), develops the essential concepts of thinking both critically and creatively. Chapter 3, Evaluating Ideas, specifically introduces and explains ideas and opinions and, in turn, provides a foundation for their critical evaluation. This chapter lays out the building blocks that are used to develop logical thought and expression and that should be present in lectures, statements, articles, speeches, textbooks, and other material that attempt to make sense, persuade, express a point of view, inform, or teach. As students begin to identify and understand these essential elements of communication and their relationships to each other, they can begin to critically evaluate the ideas presented to them therein. Once they become proficient in employing these skills, students will then be able to use them to make better decisions and solve problems more effectively (Chapter 5).

This chapter will:

- introduce and explain the concept of critical thinking.
- identify and explain the *characteristics* of *effective* critical thinking.
- point out the importance of identifying the assumptions that underlie ideas.
- explain the concept of an argument as an assertion in logical thinking.
- explain how to identify assertions, key terms, definitions, points of view, ideas.
- explain the importance of logic.
- define reasoning (inductive and deductive).
- introduce the evaluation of ideas based on an understanding of the relationship of the concepts just described.
- explain the importance of the critical assessment of evidence when evaluating ideas.
- provide a list of ways to evaluate evidence.

Suggestions for Teaching

Many of your students, like many people, believe that if an idea or opinion appears in a newspaper, magazine, or journal, then it must be true. People often believe that statements made by lawyers, doctors, journalists, college professors, and others in positions of knowledge and authority are, indeed, facts. After all, such a person must know what they are talking about, right?

Chapter 3 provides an excellent opportunity for you to explain the differences between ideas and opinions and what is factual. An understanding of these differences, as well as what underlies, supports, and influences people's ideas and opinions, is most important in to evaluating them critically. These concepts also provide important groundwork for effective decision-making and problem solving (discussed in Chapter 5).

You can use Chapter 3 to introduce your students to critical thinking and the intelligent evaluation of ideas. Consider introducing these topics with a lesson on the definitions of facts, ideas, and opinions. Even more importantly, the lesson can go on to explain how assumptions, lifestyles, background, attitudes, and experiences develop and color what become someone's ideas or opinions. Your lesson can build to the observation that what someone believes is not necessarily what is. It is up to the person receiving the information, idea, or opinion to evaluate and interpret what has been presented to him. There is an abundance of information in Chapter 3 to support this type of lesson.

Next, there are at least two obvious teaching opportunities, either or both of which are excellent to develop into lessons. Both, however, should be hands on and interactive for your students. The goal is to enable students to actively participate in their education and develop skills that they will actually use to become more productive and successful in their studies and course work.

First, you can have your students use what you have just taught them to critically analyze the statements and ideas of others. You can assign readings from newspapers, magazines, journals, or textbooks or show television news commentaries in your class. Students can then be asked to determine which statements are facts and which statements are opinions or the personal ideas of the writer or commentator. This lesson could then continue as students attempt to determine the assumptions, attitudes, and experiences that shaped and influenced the opinions and ideas that were expressed. This is an opportunity to explore a topic specific to students' majors (in a major-specific course), a topic being discussed in a linked course (for a learning community), or a hot topic in the news or on your campus.

Students should also look for evidence to support the ideas and opinions that they have read or heard. Obviously, the better and greater the amount of evidence presented, the more likely one is to be convinced that an opinion is true or correct. However, some opinions are presented as facts without any evidence at all to support them. The chapter provides an excellent explanation of the importance of such supporting evidence, as well as presenting a checklist, "Ten Ways to Evaluate Evidence," on page 46.

The second direction in which you can take your students is the development of their own original opinions. Chapter 4 also addresses this topic, presenting a wide variety of techniques and spending considerable time on brainstorming and creative idea generation. You can preview these concepts here and begin with a somewhat more structured approach that focuses on supporting evidence and assumptions.

You can begin your lesson here by assigning topics (such as cloning humans, downloading free music files, steel tariffs, etc.) to your students or have them select their own subjects about which they will develop and present their own logical opinions. Note that Chapter 3 presents an excellent sidebar (on page 44), "Common Fallacies in Logic." This provides an excellent opportunity for a short lesson that supports this assignment. The key to this lesson are the assumptions, background, and evidence that students use to support and present their opinions. This determines the quality and persuasiveness of the ideas and will be the basis on which they are judged by you as the professor in this case and, in the future, by others in and out of the classroom. Finally, to extend the lesson further, you could have the students evaluate and critique each others' opinions and supporting information in order to provide additional practice in the evaluation of ideas and develop their critical thinking skills more.

Additional Activities and Exercises

Who Is the Author? Distribute articles and editorials that you have taken from popular magazines such as *Time*, *Newsweek*, *Business Week*, *Forbes*, and the like. Ask your students to write a brief essay in which they guess as much as they can about the authors of the articles. They must support each of the author's characteristics with evidence from the article. The purpose of this exercise is to make students aware of the personal bias that can be present in some writing. That is, if the reader can determine characteristics such as the race, political affiliation, income level, or gender of the author, then the writing is less objective and unbiased.

Debate Separate your students into teams. Have teams debate issues such as music censorship, the legality or illegality of downloading music from the Internet for free, should the United States have gone to war to remove Saddam Hussein from power in Iraq?, or who should be the next president of the United States? The arguments of each team should be evaluated for logic and the quality of examples used to support them. If you are teaching in a learning community or major-specific course, you can choose a topic that is common to all students.

Emotional Appeals Have your students look for examples of emotional appeals made in magazine and newspaper articles, on television, and in advertising. Keep a record of each one in a journal or logbook, including a description and where and when it was found. Include a copy of the appeal if possible. Have students make brief presentations of their results to the class. Consider awarding a prize to the student with the most examples.

Emotions Everyone has issues that trigger strong emotional reactions in them, such as destruction of the environment or capital punishment. Have each student divide a sheet of paper into two columns. In the first column, each student should write a word or short phrase identifying such an emotional issue. In the second column, the student should write down the way in which he or she responds when the issue comes up in conversation or writing. Then each student should describe what he or she can do to remain objective when one of these emotional issues comes up. Arrange your students into small groups and have them share the objective strategies that they developed.

What's the Point? Collect six to twelve short articles from newspapers and magazines. Distribute three or four of them to each student. Have your students read the articles that they have been given and explain the purpose of the piece or identify the opinion being expressed.

Chapter 4: Creating New Ideas

The purpose of education, especially as it progresses to its higher levels, is not only to provide knowledge but also to use original thinking to create new knowledge – not in mechanical or programmed ways like a computer does but in imaginative and innovative ways.

One often thinks of creativity in terms of poetry, music, art, or literature or else in terms of great, true discoveries or innovations, such as the steam engine; manned, mechanical flight; or computers. However, creativity also helps people to solve all sorts of less revolutionary but still challenging problems, such as: the most pleasurable yet appropriate way to present a speech to a class; the best way to create an attention-getting resumé that will result in a job interview; the development of an entertaining yet effective advertising campaign; or the best way to set up a biology experiment to get valid, reliable results. In addition, the creative process, or the use and enhancement of personal and group creativity, does not have to be mysterious or unteachable. Creativity is a process that students can consciously cultivate. This chapter begins to show them how.

This chapter will:

- introduce the concept of creativity.
- explain the concept of brainstorming and its guidelines.
- present methods to use to enhance one's ability to generate ideas (with methods other than brainstorming).
- explain the importance of revision in creative and, especially, in critical thinking.

Suggestions for Teaching

Chapter 4 focuses on creativity and the processes used to generate new ideas. As these ideas are developed into their final forms, increasing structure and logic are imposed on them to mold them into their ultimate conclusions or successful solutions. However, in the initial stages of idea generation, it is more likely to be a situation where anything goes. Keep this in mind when covering these topics. This chapter can be one of the most enjoyable in the *Master Student Guide*. The first suggestion is to take advantage of the situation and have FUN!!!

Creativity can be difficult for some people. After all, creativity is, in effect, creating something out of nothing: filling up a blank page, a white computer screen, or an empty space. In fact, this process can be intimidating or even paralyzing for some. They do not know where to start. They don't know how to start. They don't think that what they have to put into these empty places will be any good. So they don't start. Your goal, with the help of this chapter, is to help your students to overcome these obstacles. Your initial goal is to get them to start.

First, try to make your students feel comfortable. Discuss the difficulty of starting any project. Talk about the intimidation of a blank, white page. Point out that they are not the only ones who experience these feelings. Explain that it can be discouraging to throw out draft after draft while searching for the one that is right. Remind them that accomplishment and success only result from action and that every conclusion must have some beginning. You are actually trying to tell your students that it is OK to be bad in the beginning, to start off wrong, to veer from one point to the next in a crooked line. Whatever it takes to get started. Hopefully, you will help them to realize that most people experience these feelings at the beginning of a new project and that there is nothing negative or wrong about having them. What is most important, though, is not being stopped by them, but overcoming them … and starting.

Next, consider explaining the technique of brainstorming to your students. Although this is a common topic, do not assume that your students are familiar with it and know how to do it. Since this is such an important technique to start the creative process, take the time to explain it fully, including its disadvantages. Chapter 4 includes a sidebar (on page 49), "Guidelines for Brainstorming," that can provide information for this lesson. Obviously, you should include a classroom activity in which your students actively practice brainstorming. This can be as simple as giving them a topic, situation, or problem and having them generate as many ideas or solutions as possible using the brainstorming techniques that they have learned. You may want to choose a topic specific to your learning community or major-specific course, if you are teaching one. (More specific activities will be given in the following section.) You can be as creative as you like here by using the blackboard, big pads of paper, colored markers, or anything else that you can dream up. Remember that you can be creative too. And remember to have fun!!

Another lesson could focus on things that help generate creativity in addition to classic brainstorming. Some of these methods can be formal techniques, such as keeping a journal of general observations, opinions, poems, ideas, pictures, songs, and anything else that comes to mind. Or they can be ways to live, such as seeking out new ideas and sources of information or exposing oneself to new experiences. The object is to increase one's creativity in all areas of one's life, so that it is easier to then generate new ideas when the need arises.

Finally, you might consider a lesson on the last part of the idea-generation process—idea revision. This is often less fun than the creative process, but it is no less important and it should not be forgotten. It is important for your students to remember that creative idea generation often produces preliminary or rough ideas and concepts. They are usually not in their polished, final form. You can choose to give an in-depth lesson on revision techniques and the importance of multiple drafts or simply review some guidelines and stress their importance, postponing a more detailed lesson until the later chapters on writing are covered. However, I would caution you not to skip the topic entirely. Many students choose to revise their work as little as possible, spending only the time and effort that they feel they need to produce work that is "good," not working through as many drafts as are needed to produce the best work they are capable of.

Additional Activities and Exercises

Traditional Brainstorm Have your students generate as many ideas as possible on a topic that you provide. Students can work alone or in small groups. Follow the brainstorming guidelines on page 49.

Possible topics: How to Make Extra Money This Week; All the Things I Want to Be When I Grow Up; Ways to Get Rid of Stress.

Charades Have your students play a game of charades. Write movie, book, and song titles on individual pieces of paper, and put them into a paper bag or bowl. Split the class into several groups. A student picks a piece of paper from the bag and acts out the title without speaking, and the other members of the group must guess what he or she is acting out. The group that can guess the title in the shortest amount of time wins that round. The purpose of this activity is to stimulate creativity and encourage students to feel more comfortable with each other.

Idea Journal Have each student keep a journal in which he or she writes down any new thoughts, ideas, or observations that he or she has had that week. Dedicate one page per week to these new ideas. This activity may be particularly useful in an online or hybrid course. You may want to check the journal weekly and administer grades for participation.

Fix-the-World Brainstorm Divide your class into groups. Each group must come up with as many ways as possible to solve some major world problem, such as pollution, the nuclear crisis in North Korea, population control, global warming, and so on. Provide each group with a large pad of paper and magic markers on which to write all of their ideas.

Something New Require each student to do something new this week. For example, go home using a different route; watch a television show that had not been seen before; shop in a new store; or go to a place, such as a lake, library, or museum, that had not been visited before. Then have each student write a short essay describing what new things they have seen or learned and why they chose that particular thing.

Timed Writing Have each student take out several blank pieces of paper. Have them start to write and continue writing without stopping for eight minutes. They can write about anything. Walk around the room and make sure that no one stops writing. Have your students discuss their results and how they felt about the exercise. As a variation, you could have them begin with a partial sentence such as: "In order to save the world, I will…"; "I am the best person because…"; or "Tomorrow, I will…".

Create a Symbol Divide your students into several groups. Tell them that every group must have a symbol that represents them to those outside the group. On a table at the front of the room, provide colored paper, feathers, buttons, magazines, ribbon, crayons, markers, glue, tape, and anything else that you want. Each group must come up with a symbol to represent it. They will have fifteen minutes to complete the project. At the end of this time, each group will explain what their symbol means to the class. The purpose of this activity is to stimulate creativity in your students.

Chapter 5: Making Decisions and Solving Problems

A student's skills in thinking culminate in his or her ability to make decisions and solve problems, in both college and his or her daily life. Students, like most others, make decisions all the time, whether they realize it or not. Even avoiding decisions is a form of decision-making. For example, a student who puts off studying for a test until the last minute or who does not get around to going to a class has actually made the decision that the test or class is not important. Or perhaps they have decided that a subject is too difficult, and they are avoiding it. In either case, the student has made a decision. And that decision will carry consequences. Therefore, a student will benefit greatly if he or she can develop a process that will allow him or her to make good decisions as often as possible.

It is important to introduce the concept of decision-making and the idea of consequences that result from those decisions to your students. It is important for students to realize that they face many decisions, both large and small, each day. These decisions are a common part of life and should *not be avoided*. By taking charge of their decisions, students take charge of their lives. You will help students to realize the many benefits of such a proactive strategy. Chapter 5 will develop a process and structure to help students make better decisions.

This chapter also explains the differences between decision-making and problem solving. Although similar in many ways, problem solving exists at an even higher level of complexity than decision-making. Problem solving calls for making a series of decisions and often answering more difficult open-ended questions. Throughout your students' college careers, just as in life, they will be called on to solve many problems. They will have to evaluate case studies, set up science experiments, solve mathematical and statistical problems, interpret literature and poetry, develop business strategies, and formulate research proposals. It is important for students to develop strong skills in solving problems so they feel comfortable in confronting the challenges that they encounter in their academic careers—and in their personal and professional lives. To help students through this process, Chapter 5 develops a four-phased problem-solving technique using Investigation, Imagination, Incubation, and Insight.

In summary, this chapter points out the importance of decision-making and problem solving and develops processes to use for each. Students should learn these processes, practice them, and enhance their skill in using them. They should work to feel more comfortable with them and then, hopefully, embrace the challenges that confront them. As they do so, they will become better equipped to achieve the academic success toward which they are working.

This chapter will:

- identify the importance of making decisions and solving problems in the lives of students.
- incorporate key elements of idea evaluation, creativity generation and enhancement, and critical thinking from the previous chapters (3 and 4) into the decision-making process.
- introduce a decision-making process that uses Investigation, Imagination, Incubation, and Insight to generate results.
- explain the importance of taking action once decisions are made and problems are solved.
- explain the differences between decision-making and problem solving.
- identify and explain the four phases of problem solving.
- introduce the benefits of solving problems in groups.

Suggestions for Teaching

As in previous chapters, an introductory lesson would serve as an appropriate starting point for this section. This lesson could explain the concepts of decision-making and problem solving, how the two differ from each other, and the benefits gained by developing these important skills. The best way to develop good decision-making skills and to improve them once they have been established is through practice. Therefore, after this brief introduction, have your students make some decisions. (Activities are suggested in the next section.)

Note: Decisions can be made and problems solved either individually or in groups. Each circumstance offers its own benefits and challenges. If time permits, you should consider allowing your students to perform some exercises or activities individually and some in groups. The same structure would then be employed for problem-solving exercises. An additional suggestion would be to have both individual students and groups make the same decision or solve the same problem. They could then compare the results, decide which decision is better, and discuss the advantages and disadvantages that they observed in using each method.

Before you assign the first decision-making activity, try to assess the composition of your class. In other words, do you feel that your students have had experience making many decisions (after all, life is made up of either making or avoiding decisions), or do you feel that they have not had many opportunities to develop this skill? For example, a single parent who has been a part of the workforce for ten years has had the opportunity to make many important decisions. In contrast, a first-year student who has graduated from high school less than a year ago has probably not had as much decision-making experience. A common decision they've all had to make is the decision to come to college. Try developing and explaining a process to them that will help guide them in their decision-making. You can share your own decision-making process or introduce the process that is explained by Engleberg and Wynn (4 I's) (see pages 59-62). If your assessment is that you have fairly experienced students, then review the decision-making steps quickly and move on to an activity. If you feel that your students are less experienced in making good decisions, spend more time developing the process.

Next, have your students practice. Assign an activity that provides a situation or scenario in which they must make a decision. For example, a situation comes up that may potentially prevent you from attending class—heavy weather report, a sick child or relative—on the day of an exam. Do you decide to go to class? In this first activity, make sure that the students strictly follow each of the steps in your chosen decision-making process (such as the 4 I's). They should follow each of the individual steps in this exercise so you are sure that they have a good understanding of the process before they begin taking shortcuts. Have the students justify their own decisions and possibly even evaluate the "quality" of each others' decisions. This activity can be assigned individually or in groups.

Remember to explain to your students that action is a key element in decision-making. Making a decision is basically making a choice about something or deciding on a course of action and then implementing that choice. One must not forget about the implementation. You have to carry out what you have decided in order to get results. The best decision will do you no good if you do not act on it. Once you are confident that your students have a better understanding of the decision-making process and have practiced making their own decisions, you can use the same format to address problem-solving skills.

A decision can often be narrowed down to a question that can be answered by yes or no or to a choice between two major options: Is the defendant guilty or not guilty? Do I vote for the Republican candidate or the Democratic one? Do I go to class today or not? Problem solving, however, is more complex. It often includes a series of decisions and/or the creative generation of unique ideas. It will address an issue such as, How do I fund my education? Or what is the best combination of marketing elements to use to reach my target audience effectively and efficiently? Solving problems effectively is best accomplished by following a series of systematic steps. Introduce a lesson that establishes such a process for your students before assigning problem-solving activities. You can explain your own preferred process or use Dewey's problem-solving steps, which are developed in Chapter 5 of the *Guide*. Since problem solving is more complex than decision-making, it is likely that fewer students will have achieved high levels of competence in this area. Therefore, it is less likely that you will be able to offer only a quick review here.

Once you feel that your students are comfortable with the process that you have taught them, have them solve some problems. (Again, either individually, in groups, or both.) If you prefer, you can have your students attempt to solve real-world problems that you can collect from newspaper or magazine articles or refer to the "Fix-the-World Brainstorm" activity in Chapter 4.

Finally, once again, remind your students that the final step in problem solving is action. In order to solve the actual problem, you must implement the solution that you have developed. One must act or the solution remains nothing more than words on a page and the problem remains unsolved.

Additional Activities and Exercises

Making Decisions Divide the class into groups. Present them with a situation that requires that a decision be made. For example, a very good job in the field that they desire is offered to them at a very high salary. However, the job is located in a city on the other side of the country. They have no friends or family in this city. A good job is also offered to them in the city in which they presently live that is near friends and family. This job also pays $10,000 less than the first position. Which job should they take?
Or a student witnesses a coworker with whom he has been friendly stealing from work on a regular basis. Should he turn him in? Each group should make a decision about the situation presented and be prepared to discuss the decision and the reasons behind it with the class.

Procrastination Divide the class into groups. Have the group members write down as many ways as possible to avoid or overcome procrastination in their studies and in their personal lives. Have each group share their ideas and strategies with the class. Record them on the blackboard or a large pad of paper. Transcribe them and distribute them to the class at the next meeting.
How Tall? Divide the class into groups. Have each group build the tallest possible freestanding structure that they can using only index cards (or straws) and tape. Set a time limit of ten or fifteen minutes. Award a prize to the group that builds the tallest structure. After the exercise, have the participants discuss how they solved the problem. Contrast the methods of the winning group with those of the other groups.

Positivity Discussion Conduct a class discussion on the benefits of proaction (versus the negative consequences of procrastination). In other words, what benefit is gained by a positive attitude and a quick, positive response to problems and decisions, as opposed to waiting as long as possible before responding or making a decision?

Problem Solving Divide the class into groups. Present a problem to the groups. For example, the group is responsible for a project in one of its classes that will be handed in for a significant grade. One member of the group has not shown up for any meetings and has not contributed very much work. The project is due in less than a week. What should they do? Or a group member needs to work in order to stay in school. How does he find a job that balances work and school? Each group should come up with what it thinks is the best solution to the problem. Each group will present its solution to the class, and then the class members will vote for the solution that they think is best.

My Problem Divide the class into groups. One student in each group should come up with an actual problem of his or her own that he or she would like to solve and is comfortable sharing with the group. Give each group twenty to thirty minutes to come up with its best solution. At the end of this time, share each problem and solution with the class. The student to whom the problem belongs should also explain whether or not he or she is satisfied with this proposed solution. As an alternative, this can be given as an individual assignment in which students write out their problem and possible solutions.

Planning to Succeed

Chapter 6: Choosing Your Life Purpose and Goals

Excellent time management is one of the most valuable skills that a student, or anyone else, can have. The *Master Student Guide* takes a broad step back, however, before focusing on the development and improvement of these skills. Chapter 6 first examines one's life purpose and the goals that result from successfully making this key decision, since a clearly defined purpose in life guides how one manages one's time. Hence, decisions that are made about what to do with one's time are directly related to the decision that has been made about what to do with one's life. Therefore, this section focuses on this important decision before examining time-management skills in the next chapter.

What is a life purpose? Answering this question so that students clearly understand what this concept means will be the professor's first task in this chapter. A purpose represents a student's overall direction and statement of her core values. It is different from a goal. A purpose, such as a desire to become wiser or accomplished at one's career, is never fully accomplished. As explained in the *Guide*, it is a journey of a lifetime, although one without a final destination. In contrast, goals (even life goals) are things that can be put on a list and crossed off as one accomplishes them. These goals are steps within the life purpose. A single life purpose can generate many goals.

"I don't know what I want to do with my life!" is a common reaction. "How can I make such a decision in one or two class periods?" might be another. However, some people spend an entire lifetime with this reaction, never answer the question, and never feel that they have done anything worthwhile with their lives. The benefits that result from the direction and focus gained by considering and answering the question of life purpose should not be underestimated.

This chapter will:

- introduce the concept of a life purpose.
- examine the differences between planning a life purpose and setting goals.
- provide a framework to help students develop their statements of life purpose.
- provide a process to help students set corresponding long-, mid-, and short-term goals that support their life purposes.
- explain the differences between long-, mid-, and short-term goals.
- Introduce the concept of a timeline to help guide the goal-setting process.
- Explore the benefits of using calendars and to-do lists to help students achieve their goals.

Suggestions for Teaching

To begin, it should be noted that it is not possible to overestimate the seriousness or importance of the material covered in this chapter. If undertaken successfully by a student, it is possible to guide, enhance, or even change the direction of her life. To that end, a primary initial objective for the professor is to communicate both the seriousness of the task at hand as well as the benefits to be derived from undertaking it. The concepts in this chapter require your student's active participation. As in many of the previously discussed topics, it is important to help students feel comfortable undertaking such a formidable and personal task.

It may be tempting to review this topic quickly and casually. However, its importance is great and its benefits are many. The commitment with which your students approach this process will be a reflection of the way in which you, the instructor, present and conduct the activities. Therefore, you should attempt to commit an appropriate amount of time for students to consider, evaluate, and contemplate various life alternatives. Present the topic carefully, devoting enough time to explain the many benefits derived from the successful completion of the chapter's activities. Actively help to guide your students through the exercises so that the results they obtain will be meaningful to them.

Remember that your students may be contemplating and discussing very personal feelings in a classroom setting. It is your goal here to help your students to feel comfortable in this environment. They can only gain from these activities if they are honest with themselves and others. They will only be honest if they feel comfortable. Sometimes an instructor will rush in to cover this topic during the first several class sessions or within the first week of the semester. It can be viewed as a good starting point upon which to build the College Success material that will follow. I would suggest, however, waiting to undertake this topic for several class sessions or for the second week or later of class (if your schedule permits) in order to allow your students to become more accustomed to and comfortable with their new environment and each other.

To begin, you will want to clearly define what is considered a life purpose, so that your students have a clear understanding of the concept when they undertake the development of their own purposes. You will probably have your students perform some type of activity in order to develop their individual statements of life purpose. Be prepared to guide them through this exercise and to frequently question their statements and the reasoning behind them. Students will often attempt to view this activity as simply an exercise to be completed and handed in, not something to live by. Their statement should adhere to the criteria that you have defined as a life purpose. For example, it should be brief and broad (not a goal) but concrete, inclusive, and so forth. Push your students to be honest with themselves. You might consider extending the lesson over two class meetings. During the first session, students will brainstorm statements of purpose, perhaps narrowing them down to two or three rough statements. Between class sessions allow them to contemplate their choices if they desire. Then during the next class session they can refine and complete their final and true statement of life purpose.

While your students are going through the process of developing a statement of purpose, do not hesitate to guide them; question their reasoning; and push them to be sincere and bold in their vision and desires. Feel free to be as elaborate as you want in this exercise. In other words, you can use large writing pads, index cards, colored markers, colored Post-it notes, signs, or anything else that you feel will help the process. And finally, of course, each student *must* write down his or her statement of life purpose. If you have the time and the resources, you might even consider printing each one out, framing it, and presenting it to each student in a small ceremony.

Finally, this chapter also introduces goal-setting to your students. It explains the differences between long-, mid-, and short-term goals and how each type supports a chosen life purpose. You should define goals and goal-setting for your students. In fact, you may have already done this when you explained the differences between a life purpose and a goal. You should also consider the use of various activities that can help teach your students how to develop and implement their own goals. Suggestions for some of these activities are given in the following section. You can use goal-setting activities within this chapter or you can use them in conjunction with the next chapter, which details time management. In other words, the successful completion of the goals that your students set (especially the mid- and short-term ones) will have an impact on the tasks that they schedule for themselves each day.

Additional Activities and Exercises

Life Purpose Prep Have each student answer the question: What is most important to me in life? Students should decide what things are most important to them and bring them the most satisfaction and happiness. These should be broad topics such as having a family, making a lot of money, freedom and independence, or expressing oneself creatively. Each chosen area will be used as a column heading on a piece of paper. Under each heading, students should write down how they think they will attain each situation.

When all students have completed this task, divide them into small groups. Have the group members review and critique each others' lists in order to help decide if the broad goals will be attainable with the steps that were identified. Each student should keep this exercise as a starting point for the development of a life purpose.

Choosing a Life Purpose Using the areas, goals, or accomplishments that were identified as most important in the preceding "Life Purpose Prep" exercise, develop a statement of life purpose. This statement should follow the definition and characteristics of a life purpose as developed in the text. It should be a broad, positive, declarative statement. It should be some purpose that will encompass a lifetime of work, development, play, and growth in the journey toward its fulfillment. As one progresses through life and gets closer to the achievement of this purpose, one should not ever fully realize or master complete accomplishment of the purpose. The instructor should review and guide students in the development of their statements. When all class members have developed appropriate life-purpose statements, each class member should stand and positively and enthusiastically declare his or her life purpose.

Life Goals This activity can be completed as a single exercise or divided into three separate exercises (each focusing on the development of a set of goals: long, mid, and short term). Have your students take out their copies of their life purposes and place them on their desks. Next, each student should develop a set of goals that he or she will work toward in the journey to fulfillment of his or her life purpose. Students should develop a separate list of long-, mid-, and short-term goals. Each goal should be consistent with a student's stated life purpose. When all students have completed their lists, divide the class members into small groups. Each group should review the members' goals in order to determine if they are consistent with and supportive of the stated life purpose. If a goal does not support the life purpose, it should be reworked until it does or be eliminated.

Lifeline Each student should create a personal timeline of his or her own life. Draw a straight line lengthwise across a sheet of paper. Place a mark at the beginning of the line to signify the student's date of birth. Place another mark an appropriate distance away to indicate the present date. Leave enough room on the line to mark events thirty to fifty years into the future, depending on one's present age. Mark significant events on the line between the birth date and the present. Finally, mark down important, anticipated future events that should occur in order to reach your life purpose and consequent goals. (Refer students to the website at http://studentsuccess.college.hmco.com/students for an interactive version of this exercise.)

Five-Year Plan Have each student develop a five-year plan. Begin by having each student write down his or her significant short- and mid-term goals for the next five years. Under each goal heading, each student should then write down what steps will need to be taken to achieve each goal.

Who Inspires You? Have each student write a one- or two-page essay about a person that he or she admires. Each student should select a person who has achieved a goal that is similar to one of the student's mid- or long-term goals. The student should include the characteristics of the admired person, the reasons why he or she chose that person, and the methods that the person used to achieve the goal.

Goal Journal Have each student select one of his or her short-term goals (a goal that can be achieved in one year or less). Each student should maintain a weekly journal record of everything that he or she does during that week that will help him or her to achieve the chosen goal. Students should keep this journal for the length of the course or semester.

Chapter 7: Managing Your Time

The management and organization of a student's time might be the most important skill that he or she can develop and master. Everyone is busy. Anyone who attends college has many demands placed on his time—time that is limited. There are only 24 hours in each day and 168 hours in each week. No matter what he does, he cannot add another hour to his day or week. Therefore, it is not so much a question of how much time a student has (all students have the same 24 hours each day), but what he does with the time that he has.

After all, it doesn't matter that a student has excellent note-taking skills if she never has any time to study her notes. It makes no difference that she can write an "A" paper if she can never find the time to sit down and actually research and write that paper. Students must learn to manage the time that they do have if they are going to achieve academic success.

This chapter will:

- explain the importance of time management.
- develop the concept of time monitoring.
- enable and encourage students to evaluate the amount of time devoted to each of their daily activities.
- help students to redistribute and balance the amount of time that *should* be spent on their daily activities.
- provide suggestions to help students use their limited time more efficiently.
- offer suggestions to help students avoid procrastination.

Suggestions for Teaching

Some people are disciplined and well organized. They are able to manage their time and their lives down to the smallest detail or event with an efficiency that maximizes their productivity. They seem to fill their days completely, finding time not only for work, school, and family, but also for play. This chapter may not be for them. Unfortunately, there are more likely fewer of these efficiently time-managing people than there are those who struggle to keep ahead of everything they believe they must get done each day. This chapter is for those who are struggling to keep up, which is probably most of us.

As the instructor, remember that, although the concepts seem simple, many people are resistant to the idea of time management. It's not that they think there is little benefit to be gained by its successful mastery. It's just that many people do not believe that they can organize their time. They just do not believe that *they* can do it.

Be prepared for two types of resistance. Many students will tell you that they are either hopelessly disorganized ("I am not an organized person. And I will never be organized.") or terribly overwhelmed ("There is simply too much to do. I will never be able to fit it all in."). They will tell you, basically, that this is never going to work for them. In fact, for every situation your students are in—if they are student-athletes, adult learners with families or full-time jobs, transfer students, online students, commuter students—there will be some reason why this will not work. This will be the first challenge that you need to overcome. You must convince your students that anybody can manage his or her time better and add more balance to their lives. Anybody can use these techniques to become better organized and more successful in the things that are important to him or her. Then you must deliver on this promise.

You can think of the activities that follow as a construction project. You are teaching your students how to build a better, less stressful, more successful life (or schedule, at least). The first step in this construction project must be the assessment of what your students spend their time doing each day, all day long. In order to find out what activities consume the most time, where time is being wasted, and what is being left out, students must know exactly what they are doing. Therefore, your students must track or monitor their daily activities for some period of time, typically a week.

The *Master Student Guide* calls this step "time monitoring" and offers strategies and a process to complete this part of the project (direct students to the website for more information and practice with time monitors). However, you can use any method to guide your students as they track their activities as long as it meets several criteria. First, they need to write down their activities. Time monitoring results in a large amount of information that needs to be organized and analyzed systematically in order to yield results in the subsequent stages of the project. Working from memory will not be possible. In addition, try not to make it burdensome to monitor these activities. Students can even use a notepad or index cards as long as they collect accurate information. However, keep in mind that many of the students who most need to improve their time-management skills may not be very well organized. Therefore, you might want to provide some type of assessment instrument or worksheet (with a day broken down into one-hour segments). In this way you can ensure that students account for each hour of their day without gaps, including time that they spend sleeping, as well as help to convey the seriousness of the exercise.

Encourage your students to record their activities as soon as they do them, or soon after. This is not an activity that will be performed in the classroom from memory. This is the cornerstone of the time-management project, and it must be accurate. We often spend more or less time on certain projects than we think we do. The purpose of this exercise is to eliminate any misconceptions about how students spend their time so that they can realistically balance and reschedule their time later in the project. Therefore, time monitoring must be done in real time, so to speak. As a result, this topic cannot be completed in a single class session. Obviously, it will take one to two weeks to perform time monitoring that will yield useful information upon which to build.

Finally, your students must be honest. They cannot record eight hours of sleep time because they believe that this is the accepted amount when they actually sleep for ten hours most nights. If they spend an hour playing with and reading to their children each day, this must be recorded. This time cannot be ignored because students think that you will perceive it as leisure or play time. The purpose of time management is not simply to eliminate activities from a student's life. Time management is undertaken to provide organization, determine where time might be wasted, and develop a schedule that allows one to do all of the things that one must get done. In order to build a schedule that leads to balance and success in all areas of a student's life, one must have honest and accurate information to analyze and organize.

Now that your students have assembled their information, they are ready to analyze and organize. Before they do this, however, they should review the life goals that they established in Chapter 6. As a matter of fact, your students should take out a copy of these goals and refer to them as they schedule their time. First, have your students map out an entire week. (They can use a blank set of the preprinted sheets that were used for time monitoring.) Begin by filling in all those things that absolutely *have* to be done, for example, the time that is spent in class each day, the time spent sleeping and eating, or the time spent taking a child to daycare.

Next, have your students add in the things that they *should* be doing. They would fill in the time that they study, for example. They would calculate the amount of time that they should be studying and map this out over the course of a week. Your students should compare these activities to the goals that they have established for themselves. They should directly support these goals, or your students should reconsider whether these activities should be undertaken. Finally, your students can evaluate how much time is left and where it is located so they can now schedule other activities accordingly. Hopefully, some "free" time was left because leisure, relaxation, or break time is also important and should not be left out.

Be prepared for some students to argue that such a tightly managed schedule forces them to give up freedom in their lives. You could point out that a little bit of organization builds efficiency in the use of their time and thereby creates freedom. Whereas before there was too much to get done and little time for play or free time, now this new efficiency allows for a better chance to get everything done and an opportunity to schedule some play time. True, some spontaneity may be sacrificed, but much more is ultimately accomplished with less effort.

Now that your students have constructed their new schedules, review the tools that they can use to maintain their new organized lives, such as daily and weekly planners, to-do lists, index cards, personal digital assistants, computer software, and perhaps the most effective (but least used) strategy of simply saying no sometimes. Chapter 7 covers many of these topics. You may choose to end your lessons on this topic or conduct a discussion of one of the greatest obstacles to successful time management: procrastination. Chapter 7 concludes by addressing this subject. Remind your students, however, that ultimately the best and only way to overcome this obstacle and be successful is to "Just do it!"

Additional Activities and Exercises

What I Can Do Without Divide the class into groups. Have each group brainstorm to create a list of nonessential activities that could be eliminated from their lives. For example, socializing with friends for an hour each day could be cut back to half an hour. Calling a friend each day could be cut back to calling three times per week or e-mailing every day and calling once per week. Have each group share its list with the class.

How to Say No Conduct a class discussion on how to say no to people. Focus on strategies to say no to people who can make it difficult to say no to them, such as parents, spouses, or close friends. Also address how to say no when you would like to say yes. After the discussion, present different situations to your students in which they should say no, and select a student to role-play how they would now handle each situation.

Inventory of Importance Have each student create a list of those things that are most important in his or her life and/or things that he or she most want to accomplish. Next to each item on the list, write down those activities that will have to be done daily or weekly in order to accomplish these important things. Include the amount of time that will be needed for each of these activities.

Procrastination Divide the class into groups. Have the group members write down as many ways as possible to avoid or overcome procrastination in their studies and in their personal lives. Have each group share their ideas and strategies with the class. Record them on the blackboard or a large pad of paper. Transcribe them and distribute them to the class at the next meeting.

Ideal Schedule Have each student create his or her ideal schedule. For example, if one is least tired in the morning and would study best at this time, schedule this activity for the morning on the ideal schedule. If it would be most convenient or affordable to take care of children in the morning and take courses at night or in the afternoon, place this activity appropriately on the ideal schedule. This now becomes a guide toward which to work in planning one's future daily activities.

Daily To-Do Conduct a lesson on how to develop, use, and maintain a daily or weekly calendar and a to-do list. Include the importance of prioritization, and so on. Have each student properly use such a daily or weekly calendar or planner for at least one week. At the end of this time period, conduct a class discussion focused on how well or poorly it worked for your students and the reasons why it was or was not successful.

Build an Academic Schedule Since your students are enrolled in college courses, this should be one of the priorities in their lives. Before they build an overall time schedule, have them construct a schedule that includes only those academic activities that they must complete and in which they must participate to achieve success in college. Students must include accurate estimates of the time needed daily or weekly for each activity. This becomes the basis for the required or most important activities that must be included on the master calendar.

Time Journal Have each student keep a daily journal in which he or she notes the times that he or she has successfully maintained his or her planned schedule and those times when he or she has not. Students should also record the reasons why they were not able to complete all of their scheduled activities. Conduct periodic discussions focused on the successes and failures recorded in the journals and the methods, strategies, and obstacles that resulted in each.

Goals versus Schedule Have each class member take out the daily/weekly schedule that he or she has developed and the list of goals that he or she compiled when working in the previous chapter. Students should compare the activities on the time schedule with the goals on the list. The activities should support some goal on the list. Consider eliminating activities that do not support or are in conflict with some goal.

Bad Habits Divide your class into groups. Have each group compile a list of the bad habits that cause the group members to waste time. For each time-wasting habit, have the group develop a strategy to eliminate the habit. Have each group share its list of habits and strategies with the class.

Chapter 8: Choosing Your Major and Planning Your Career

Two of the most important decisions that people will make in their lives are where to go to college and what to study when they get there. At this point, your students have made the first decision, and they are enrolled in your course (whatever that might be) and seated in your classroom. They are then left with the second decision: What to choose for their major course of study? Some may have already chosen their majors. Some may not have done so yet. Many of those who have already selected a major will change that major at some point during their college careers. In some cases, this may even require changing schools.

So, why do students attend college? The answer, in almost all cases, is to get an education. And they are satisfied that the college they have chosen will provide that education. However, a satisfying and lucrative career is often the actual goal of this education, as the *Master Student Guide* points out in Chapter 8.

In order to choose the correct major, it is important for a student to clearly define his career goals. Then he or she can plan his or her education and a strategy for reaching these goals effectively. As a result, choosing a major is really the final topic that should be addressed in this area. First, a student should undertake an assessment of his skills, both those that he presently possesses and those that he would like to develop and acquire. Next, he should choose a career and career goals. Then he should develop a career plan. Meanwhile, he should explore different options, work at various jobs or internships, and undergo a period where he tries things out. As he clarifies and more solidly determines his goals and career plan, he should then choose a major that accommodates both the skills that he has and the career that he wants. Chapter 8 maps out a strategy that will help students to do this.

This chapter will:

- explain the relationship between skills, job, and career.
- define and compare content and transferable skills.
- provide methods to help students assess their skills.
- discuss the difficulties and obstacles in choosing a major.
- explain the importance of flexibility when choosing a major.
- offer methods to help choose a career.
- explain how to create a career plan.
- provide a four-year strategy for career planning (see checklist).

Suggestions for Teaching

As you begin your first discussion of the topics in this section with your students, remember that many students will believe that choosing the right major course of study will help them to get a good job and will, in turn, lead to a satisfying and successful career. You should first explain that choosing a major is not the first step in planning a career. It is actually the last step, as previously pointed out. An inventory or assessment of skills that a student possesses, along with activities of interest, is the starting point, followed by the development of career goals and, ultimately, a career plan. Finally, a major course of study is chosen that will enable one to begin the employment journey that fulfills this career plan. The *Master Student Guide* has outlined an effective process to take students through these steps.

First, however, as in other sections that deal with broad life decisions, you might need to overcome resistance by your students. They may express the feeling that this is such a large and overwhelming task that it cannot be accomplished in several class meetings. True, it is an important decision that may affect the next several years, if not the rest, of their lives. But if one never takes on a serious and honest evaluation of one's needs and desires in life, then one will not ever be able to make a good decision about these needs and desires. This chapter provides a series of activities that break down the large and broad decision into smaller and more manageable tasks.

Besides, students do not have to choose a major in their first semesters. Even if they attend a college that requires them to declare a program of study in their very first semester, they can always change their major later. Make sure that your students understand that there is *nothing wrong with changing their majors.* Many students do this. In fact, many people change careers several times in their lives. The reality is that what one *expects* of a job or project is often different than what one experiences when one is actually working at that job or performing that project. It is OK to change your mind!!

A student's college experience should be a time to experiment and try things out, most importantly, different courses of interest and areas of study that might lead to different careers. A four-year college program provides an excellent opportunity to clarify ideas, desires, and goals. Therefore, some would even argue that a major should not be declared until the end of a student's first year or within her second year. After all, even if you change careers several times, you will spend many years of your life pursuing each one. And the goal of a career should not only be monetary success, but also personal satisfaction and growth. It is important for your students to understand this as they set their career goals and work to establish their career plans. As a result of these multiple and sometimes conflicting goals, a period of assessment and experimentation should result in a better decision.

Not all students proceed directly from high school to college or are enrolled in traditional four-year programs. Many students attend two-year colleges or are enrolled in accelerated programs in which they earn a four-year degree in less than four years. While the same processes of experimentation and assessment are still important, these processes will need to be accelerated in these situations. Many nontraditional students are returning to higher education after long periods away from the academic world, and many are changing careers. This may cause concern and anxiety as to whether they have made the correct decisions. Careful consideration of their choices and opportunities using the activities in this chapter, along with your support and guidance, can help to reassure them and allow them to confidently reevaluate their decisions if needed.

As stated previously, the first step or activity is a skills and activity assessment. Many formal instruments that have been developed specifically for this purpose can be used (see Additional Activities and Exercises for some suggestions). Or you can use an informal process that uses a pen and paper or a journal. The key, though, is for students to be honest. Only an honest evaluation will lead to decisions that result in true career and personal satisfaction in later years. If your students are not being honest with themselves, then they are simply completing the assignment to hand in to you and move on to the next one, not for their own gain.

Your students should assess the skills that they possess now, as well as those skills that they want to obtain and believe that they will or should learn over the course of their education. In addition, in preparation for setting career goals, your students can develop a list of activities in which they are interested and that they enjoy. This will help guide the research that they will do in this next step.

Next, Chapter 8 will help your students to establish career goals and develop a career plan. In other words, in what field would they like to work? Or more basically, what would they like to do? Remind your students that their opportunities are wide open; they should not limit themselves at the beginning of this process. They can achieve the best results if they start this part of the process with an open mind: I can do anything that I want. Now is their chance! They should look for that career that will bring them satisfaction and happiness.

You may encounter resistance here (or even panic), especially from your nontraditional students who have returned to college specifically to change careers and who believe that they have already made these decisions. These activities also provide these students with one more opportunity to evaluate their decisions and change them if necessary. (Remember: there is nothing wrong with changing your mind.) After all, they have made the most difficult decision: to change their career. Now it is just a matter of making sure that they have decided to change it to the right thing.

If your students are convinced that all careers are open to them and that they can do anything, the next step is to narrow down their possible choices and eliminate careers in which they are clearly not interested. These steps involve research in order to gain a better understanding of the opportunities available from the shorter, revised career lists. Eventually, your students will be able to narrow down their career choices and develop them into career goals and a career plan. Finally, the selection of a major will then be an obvious choice that supports their plan and their goals.

Additional Activities and Exercises

Career Services Invite a representative from the Career Services department to visit your class to discuss career choices or take your class to the office of the Career Services department to discuss career choice and the resources available in the office.

Skills Assessment Have each student develop a comprehensive list of skills that he or she possesses, including both content and transferable skills. He or she should create a second list of skills that he or she will possess by the time he or she completes college and that he or she wants to learn in the near future. These lists will be used in the student's search for an appropriate career in later exercises.

What Do I Want to Do with My Life? Divide the class into groups. Distribute a large piece of paper to each student and magic markers to each group. Each student should write down all of the things that he or she wants to do in his or her life. Include both career and non-career-related things. When this part of the exercise is completed, have the students put each item into one of three categories: Career, Result of Career Success, and Outside of Career. Upon completion of this part of the exercise, have each student explain to the other members of his or her group how each thing is related to the others and/or how it will be achieved.

Jobs in My Field After each student has researched career fields and settled on one or several possible fields of interest, have him or her develop a list of actual job titles and descriptions in each field of interest. Include at least six to twelve jobs in each field of interest. Possible sources of research include classified ads, the library, the U.S. Department of Labor's SCANS report, the college's Career Services department, and the *Occupational Outlook Handbook.*

Life Collage Divide the class into small groups. Distribute a large, blank piece of paper to each student. Distribute magazines, glue, and several pairs of scissors to each group. Each student should create a collage of pictures that represent his or her life goals and accomplishments. When the collages are completed, each student should explain what the pictures represent to the other group or class members (depending on the size of the class).

Career Plan Once a potential career has been identified by each student, have students create a plan outlining all of the steps that will be needed to achieve success in that field. Have each student construct a plan, picture, or map illustrating these steps with some representation of career success as the final destination.

College Career Plan This is a variation on the career plan that is explained earlier. In this case, instead of creating a map or picture of all the steps of one's entire career path, only those things that must be undertaken in college to move toward one's chosen career are included. This activity provides somewhat more focus on the near-term tasks needed to set one's career plan in motion and can be less intimidating than mapping out a twenty- to thirty-year career.

Career/Informational Interview Have each student interview someone who is presently employed in the career field in which he or she has decided that he or she would like to work. Students should try to find out such things as what the subjects like and dislike about their careers, what needs to be done to be successful, what the work requirements and obligations are, and so on. Each student should summarize the interview in a short paper that will be submitted.

Career Portfolio Have each student begin a portfolio of achievements, awards, and examples of work that showcases his or her skills. The portfolio can begin as a formal folder or CD in which the student will accumulate examples of outstanding work and accomplishments throughout his or her college and/or employment history. Although there will be little to include during a student's first semester, each student should be required to keep his or her best exams, projects, and essays from this semester. The purpose is to develop the habit of keeping samples of his or her best work. Early work can be replaced later as better examples are obtained as skills and talents are developed and refined.

Find a Mentor Have each student find a career mentor, that is, someone who works in the same field that the student has chosen to pursue. Students should meet or speak with their mentors on a regular basis in order to gain advice and understanding about the career that they have selected. Students should keep a journal throughout the semester to record important ideas from these meetings and discussions, as well as their feelings about them.

Reading and Note-Taking with a Purpose

Chapter 9: Using Three Steps to Active Reading

Academic success is the result of thinking critically, answering questions, solving problems, and processing information, among many other skills. All of these processes usually involve some amount of information collection. How do students collect information? Much of it is done by reading. Reading is such an important aspect of almost all college courses that all students can benefit from the review of this chapter. It can be especially helpful to those teaching in learning communities since it can easily be adapted into one or two lessons using selected readings from the actual course work used in the academic class to which it is attached.

Reading plays a role in the success of so many aspects of students' lives that students often must spend a great deal of time on this pursuit. However, time spent reading is just one activity that makes up a student's busy day. Therefore, it is important to do it efficiently yet effectively. Students should work to minimize the amount of time spent reading as much as this is possible, while at the same time maximizing retention and understanding. In order to do this, a student must become an active reader. In other words, a student needs to become an active participant in the process. Although reading appears to be a passive activity, a student must learn to actively participate mentally, possibly even physically (as Chapter 9 will point out).

Chapter 9 will identify and explain the three steps that will turn a student into an active reader. These three steps will develop a process that transforms the reader into an active participant by having her: ask questions about what she reads; read to answer these questions; and reflect on the answers (to ensure and increase understanding).

This chapter will:

- identify the characteristics of active reading.
- introduce and explain the three steps needed to develop the skill of active reading.

Suggestions for Teaching

College life requires a huge amount of reading, followed by retention, analysis, and critical thinking. Fortunately, all of your students will know how to read. However, it is easy to become overwhelmed by the volume of reading needed to keep up with lectures and assignments, while also balancing commitments to athletic teams, a job (possibly a full-time one), perhaps parental responsibilities, friends, and everything else competing for a student's attention.

You can first point out to your students that you are not talking about reading for pleasure or leisure. This is a specific type of reading. This is reading with a purpose, reading for content and understanding. To be successful at this type of reading, one should approach reading as a process or a series of steps. One will no longer open to the first page and simply read through to the last page and hope that one remembers something. The reader will now actively participate in the process. It may appear that proceeding through the steps will make reading take longer. However, reading something once with great comprehension and understanding reduces the need to go back to the material in the future. Thus, successful mastery of the active reading process actually saves time in the long run.

Many of your students, especially those who are returning to school after many years and have not touched a textbook in some time, will not be familiar with the concept of active reading. Chapter 9 lays out each step of the process clearly and in detail. Although your students can obviously read, you should approach the concept of active reading as a new skill for them. Explain each part of the process as if they are hearing it for the first time. They may, in fact, be reading this way for the first time in their lives. As you explain each topic, also point out the benefits gained by preparing to read and reading in this way.

Finally, just as you want your students to participate actively in their reading, so too should they actively participate in these lessons. As you teach your students each of the steps, consider having them complete an exercise in which they perform that step using some actual reading material, preferably something from one of their courses. The "Experiment with a Strategy from This Chapter" section in Chapter 9 provides an excellent series of exercises to do this. It can be broken down into separate activities to be completed after each individual step in the active reading process is taught. Or it can be used as a single comprehensive review lesson to ensure understanding upon completion of all three steps and the many elements within them.

Additional Activities and Exercises

Reading Obstacles Divide the class into small groups. Have the group members discuss the distractions and obstacles that prevent them from concentrating and comprehending information when reading. Each group should create a list of these distractions and obstacles. Then each group should come up with ways to remove the distractions and overcome the obstacles. This exercise can also be conducted as a class discussion.

Previews Assign a chapter from the textbook that you use for your course and plan to cover in the near future. Or have each student pick a chapter that he or she has not yet read from the textbook from one of his or her other courses. This tactic might work especially well in a learning-community-based course or major-specific course, where a common text is shared. Or assign an article of significant length from a major news periodical. Have your students skim or briefly look over the chapter or article. Once they have completed this preview, they should list or outline the key or main points of the chapter or material. This preview list will act as a guide to improve their comprehension and retention. As students improve their previewing skills, they will be able to focus their reading by mentally previewing material without recording the key points prior to reading.

Focused Reading Have each student select a chapter that he or she has not yet read from one of their textbooks or assign a long article from a major news periodical. Students should read for five minutes. At the end of this time, have the students stop reading and write a short paragraph summarizing and explaining what they have just read. Repeat this focused reading and forced recall two or three more times.

Questions Assign a chapter from the textbook that you use for your course and plan to cover in the near future. Or have each student pick a chapter that he or she has not yet read from the textbook from one of his or her other courses. Or assign an article of significant length from a major news periodical. Before reading the chapter or article, have each student develop a list of questions that he or she believes he or she should answer in order to understand the material. Begin by developing several questions without skimming or previewing the chapter or material. Then have each student preview the material briefly to complete his or her list of questions.

Answer the Questions This exercise is a continuation of the preceding activity titled "Questions." Have each student read the chapter or material that was assigned in this previous activity. Then have the students answer the questions that they had prepared in this previous activity.

Studying Your Textbook Divide the class into groups. Each group member should explain to the other members how he or she reads and studies from his or her textbook. When all members have shared their methods, each group should create a list of those methods that they believe are most effective. Each group should share their list of methods with the class.

Listen to the News Each student should watch one half-hour news broadcast. At the conclusion of the broadcast, the student should summarize as much as he or she can remember from the entire broadcast. If you want to ensure that the students wait until the end of the broadcast to write their summaries, you can record one of the news broadcasts and have your students view it in the classroom, writing the summary as a classroom exercise when the broadcast is finished.

Reading Journal Have your students keep a journal record of all material that they read for several weeks. Students should note which reading sessions were productive or unproductive and try to determine the reasons for each. Upon completion of the designated time period, students should share their results with the class.

Mark the Book Many students do not write in their college textbooks. However, they have purchased these books; they belong to them. Encourage your students to make notes in and mark up their textbooks as a way to increase understanding of the material. You could even allow your students to spend fifteen minutes reading a chapter from one of their textbooks and encourage them to make notes in the book.

Chapter 10: Becoming a Flexible Reader

Reading is an activity that varies depending upon both the type of material that is read and the purpose for which it is being read. Students do not need to read everything with the same level of attention or even the same speed. In other words, there is a certain amount of flexibility that a successful student uses in order to save time when possible and pay more attention when needed.

Not all reading material that a student encounters in college is the same. There is a huge difference between reading a mathematics or statistics textbook and reading a play by Shakespeare or a story by Ernest Hemingway. The way in which each is read through should be different. Students can be more efficient, more effective, and ultimately more successful if they recognize the different types of reading material that they encounter and actually adapt the way that they read to the different materials and the different purposes required of each. The goal is for students to learn how to build flexibility into their reading.

This chapter will:

- explain the 80/20 principle and how it can be applied to a student's reading.
- introduce the concept of a reading plan and teach students how to create one.
- develop strategies to adjust reading pace to the requirements of different materials being read.
- develop strategies to overcome confusion encountered while reading (see the sidebar on page 126).
- help students to develop skills to read successfully across the curriculum.
- remind students of the benefits of a strong vocabulary.
- provide a checklist of common prefixes, roots, and suffixes to help build a stronger vocabulary.

Suggestions for Teaching

All of your students know how to read. They will tell you this. And they will demonstrate it for you. As a result, many students believe that they face only two obstacles in terms of the reading required of them in college. First, they must find the time to complete the large volume of reading encountered in each class. Second, they need to understand the (often) complex subject matter that they must read.

While these two challenges are real, you must first point out to your students that the way to overcome these potential obstacles is to adapt the way that they read to the material that is being read. In other words, there are different ways to read different types of reading material. Flexibility is key when reading for understanding and comprehension at the college level. As a student learns what types of material or sections of text can be skimmed, how to spot clues that signal important information, and how to develop questions that should be answered through reading, among other skills he or she will eventually be able to lower the total amount of time spent reading and studying and increase his or her comprehension of the material read.

Flexible reading often is a skill that needs to be taught and developed. Many students have not approached reading in this way. After you have explained this concept to your students and convinced them of its benefits, Chapter 10 will provide you with much material to teach them the various skills needed to identify the differences within the reading material encountered in their course work and then to evaluate the material and determine the pace of reading required as well as the skills needed to most efficiently understand the material. The chapter then develops a series of different skills to be used by students on various types of reading materials.

The only way to become proficient at a new skill is to practice it. Therefore, it is important that you provide an opportunity for your students to practice what you have taught them. You can hand out several sections from a textbook for them to use. Have them prepare to read. That is, develop the questions that they think they will need to answer from reading this assignment. Then have them determine what type of reading needs to be done, what pace they should use, and any special strategies they should use to get the most out of their reading assignment. You can stop and evaluate their responses and strategies here or the students can continue on to read. After completion of the reading assignment, you can evaluate their level of comprehension. Remember that the material that you choose for them to read does not have to be from a subject they are familiar with. The purpose of building flexibility into their reading is to increase their efficiency and, more importantly, their understanding of unfamiliar material.

As an alternative exercise, you can have your students read sections from a chapter of a textbook that they are using in one of their actual courses. This can help to make the exercise even more useful for your students. If you are using sections of the *Master Student Guide* to support one of their academic subjects, simply have your students use part of their next chapter as a class exercise. Or if the *Guide* is used within a learning community, select one of the academic subjects within the community and use sections from the chapter of the corresponding text for the exercise. As always, it is extremely important to complete the exercise in the classroom in order to guide your students to mastery of the new concept. It will be less effective to explain these skills and then leave your students to utilize them on their own, without reinforcement.

Finally, Chapter 10 concludes with sections on vocabulary building. A strong vocabulary is an extremely important tool in effective written and oral communication. It is tempting to omit this section at the college level. I would urge you to consider including it in your curriculum if possible, especially if you are using the textbook as part of a First-Year Experience course, although many other courses would benefit from an enhanced vocabulary as well.

Any type of review of the vocabulary skills in Chapter 10 would be helpful. The most benefit would be gained, however, if you could somehow include vocabulary building throughout an entire semester. There is a Connecticut teacher who teaches advanced English classes to sixth-, seventh-, and eighth-graders. She requires extensive vocabulary work. The students must learn the definitions of thirty new words every two to three weeks. They take short quizzes three to four days each week.

Most of the quizzes are cumulative throughout the entire year. That is, the students are required to know the words from the first week on the last quiz in June. It is an incredibly challenging undertaking, but most of the students are successful. By the end of the year they have increased their vocabulary by 450 words. In three years they know almost 1,500 new words. Most of these students are very good, if not excellent, writers.

I am not advocating such a huge and complex undertaking in your course. However, if you can help to increase the vocabulary skills of your students a little bit, you will make them much better communicators and help to develop a skill that will benefit them across the college curriculum.

Additional Activities and Exercises

Reading Plans Have each student create a specific reading plan for each of the courses that he or she is taking this semester. Review each student's set of plans to ensure that they are accurate and realistic.

What's Important Divide your class into small groups. Assign a section of a chapter from your textbook that has not yet been covered. Or distribute an article of significant length from a major news periodical. Each student should read the chapter section or the magazine article. The students in each group should then decide what was *not* important and could have been skimmed quickly in their readings. Each group should then report its findings and the reasons that the material was determined to be unimportant to the class.

Tell Me What You've Read Divide your class into pairs of students. Distribute copies of recent articles from newspapers and magazines to your students. Make sure that each student in a pair receives different articles than his or her partner. Have each student read one of his or her articles. When both students in a pair have finished reading, the partners should take turns explaining what they have read to the other. Repeat this activity several times.

Word Parts Have your students review the checklist of common prefixes, word roots, and suffixes found on page 131-133 in Chapter 10. Distribute copies of recent articles from newspapers and magazines to your students. Give several different articles to each student. Have your students identify all the words that they can find in each article using the prefixes, roots, and suffixes from this list. Award extra points to the student who has identified the most words.

Personal Dictionary Have each student use a journal or small notebook to create a personal dictionary of new and unfamiliar words. Whenever your students read for school or pleasure throughout the semester, they should record any words whose meanings they do not know. They should look up the definitions and write them next to the words, creating a personal dictionary that will help to expand their vocabularies.

Chapter 11: Using Seven Tools for Powerful Notes

One of the most valuable skills that any student can have is the ability to take clear and effective notes that support and enhance the learning process. This is not simply transcribing what one hears or reads. It is economically recording important information that one will be able to refer back to at a later date in order to remember facts and essential opinions, to serve as a basis for study and review, and to enhance understanding.

Anyone can write things down, but powerful and effective note-taking is a refined skill that requires attention and practice. While there are many specific methods, strategies, hints, and guidelines for effective note-taking, Chapter 11 begins with a broader approach. (Specific methods and strategies are developed in Chapters 12–14.) This chapter introduces a basic structure for note-taking. It prepares students with a basic series of steps that can be used with any of the methods that are developed in the following chapters. It develops the basic foundations of preparation and organization upon which the details of a student's preferred note-taking method can be built. This chapter addresses initial preparation by students before they attend a lecture or open a textbook, the choice of a specific technology to be used for note-taking, the importance of listening, note-taking abbreviations, the use of key words, the development of levels of ideas, and prediction of test questions as a note-taking tool.

This chapter will:

- introduce and explain the seven steps of effective note-taking.
- suggest ways to deal with a fast-talking lecturer.
- teach students to predict test questions in order to focus note-taking more effectively.

Suggestions for Teaching

One of the themes developed throughout the *Master Student Guide for Academic Success* is the idea that students should take personal responsibility for the navigation of their own academic journey and its ultimate success. Perhaps that is nowhere more important than when a student is taking notes from a professor's lecture, from a textbook, or from any other media or situation. It is in large part the quality of those notes (and what the student is able to take from them later) that determines that student's academic success. Those notes are only as good (useful) as what goes into them. And what goes into them is the student's responsibility.

As instructor, it is your responsibility to communicate the importance of this skill to your students. You must convince them that they must be positive and proactive about note-taking. It is up to the student to take good notes that will be useful to him or her in the future. Although it would be ideal for each instructor to enhance the quality of her lectures for the utmost ease of her students' note-taking, not all instructors will do so. It is still the ultimate responsibility of the student to compensate in these situations and take notes of high quality. Each student is responsible for his or her own education and academic success. Professors who speak fast or with a foreign accent, jump from topic to topic, or do not write on the blackboard do not provide excuses for poor notes and low grades. Rather, they are challenges to be overcome. You, along with the *Master Student Guide*, will teach them how to do this.

As you review Chapter 11, you will see that it provides a clear structure and set of guidelines to help improve students' note-taking skills. Use the methods and hints developed by these seven steps to construct the foundation upon which your students will then select a specific process of note-taking that they would like to try.

Once you have completed the seven steps in this chapter (or at any point that you feel is appropriate), have your students practice the skills that you have taught them. As always, have them use what you have taught them while you are available to guide them and check their work. Often, the activity here will be straightforward and simple. Have your students take some notes, then review them to see if they have correctly used some or all of the initial skills in the seven steps. They can take notes from one of your lectures. Or you can implement this lesson across the curriculum. Choose another course in their curriculum, and have them take notes for an entire lecture and then submit those notes to you for review. This will allow you to critique your students' new skills in a more realistic environment with a professor who might be less "sympathetic" to their new skills than you are.

Remember that your students are more likely to continue to use these new skills if they feel that they have mastered them and if they believe that they are of benefit to them. Simply lecturing on these skills without actual practice and help in implementing them will not encourage most students to keep using them. They will only see them as a lesson to be completed and then from which to move on. It is important that your students see these skills as an important opportunity to help themselves move further on their journey to academic success.

Additional Activities and Exercises

How to Take Good Notes Divide the class into groups. Have each group develop a list of ways in which students can take effective notes. Each group should share its list with the class. This activity can also be conducted as a class discussion.

How to Overcome a Fast Lecture Conduct a class discussion that develops a list of strategies that students can use to take effective notes when confronted by a professor who speaks very fast or lectures in a disorganized manner.

How Do You Take Notes? Have each student write a short essay describing the typical process that he or she uses to take notes. Each student should also critique each step of the process that he or she uses.

Test Questions Have each student bring in notes from the last several sessions of one of their classes. Or use the notes that your students have taken from the last several lectures that you have given. From these notes, have each student develop a list of test questions that he or she believes the instructor might ask on the next exam. The ultimate purpose of this exercise is to begin to train students to anticipate future test questions while they are taking notes. In other words, as students are listening to a lecture and taking notes, they are anticipating the future test question that will result from the lecture material and they include that question in their notes for future reference.

Shorthand Lecture The purpose of this activity is to help your students develop and practice using their own shorthand system of abbreviations for note-taking. During your next classroom lecture, have your students take notes using as many abbreviations and shortened sentences as possible. Or have them perform this activity in the next available lecture of one of their core courses. In either case, review the notes that the students have taken to ensure that they are still understandable and will still make sense several weeks in the future.

Silly Lecture Conduct a lecture on some silly topic that is unrelated to any subject that you are covering. For example, explain how to tie a bow tie, discuss your favorite novel and how it changed your life, tell the story of the funniest things that your children have ever done, or discuss any silly, fun topic. Have your students take notes on this lecture. Briefly review the quality of these notes. The purpose of this activity is to focus students on the mechanics of note-taking, not on the subject matter. Therefore, by lecturing on some silly topic, students will be less focused on the "importance" of the material presented and can concentrate on the proper format with which to take notes.

Textbook Notes Have your students take notes while they are reading the next chapter in your class or the next chapter in one of their core courses. Review the quality of these notes.

Chapter 12: Notes: Experimenting with the Cornell Format

Chapter 12 suggests that a student can think of her notes as a textbook that she creates herself, but one that she can personalize so that it best meets her own needs. One of the key advantages of this personalized book is that it is written in the format that is best understood by its creator. Hopefully, by using her own words, structure, and thought processes, the "writer" creates a book of notes that leads to better understanding than definitions copied directly from a textbook or professor's lecture. Each student also has the freedom to experiment with different methods of note-taking in order to create that customized book that is best for her.

The first of several methods that the *Master Student Guide* introduces is the Cornell Format in Chapter 12. As was the case with the note-taking methods introduced in Chapters 13 and 14, this method takes students out of the traditional note-taking format. Instead of transcribing the professor's words or translating his words into the student's own on the page, this method makes note-taking more purpose focused. In other words, the main purpose of taking notes should be the creation of a set of notes that are most effective and useful for studying. The Cornell Format focuses on this ultimate goal by setting up the page upon which notes are recorded using a unique structure that should make later review and study much easier.
Students, like everyone else, are often resistant to change, including change in their method of taking notes. This new method of note-taking, with its ease and simplicity, might lessen some of this resistance. It might open up students to try other new methods of note-taking and thereby find the one that is the best fit for them and enables them to study and learn most effectively.

This chapter will:

- introduce students to the Cornell Format of note-taking.
- explain the advantages of studying when using the Cornell Format.
- teach students how to use the cue column and summary area (when using the Cornell Format).

Suggestions for Teaching

It is a fact that people do not like change. Even in studying and taking notes, many students do not like change. Students who are performing well academically see no reason to change what appears to be working well for them. Students who are not doing well in their studies often believe that the last thing that they need to do is take time to learn a new way to take notes when they could use that time to study. However, an investment of time now could generate greater academic benefits in the future. And in the former case, the "good" student may take adequate notes now, but he might be able to learn a new way of note-taking that is even more effective and efficient than his present method. Thus, he becomes an even better student and creates more "free" time for himself to manage to his best advantage.

The purpose of this chapter, along with Chapters 13 and 14, is to get your students to try taking notes in a new way. It is important in school, and in life, to try new things. One will not know if something better is out there if one does not try something new. It is your goal to introduce the Cornell Format of note-taking to your students and ensure that they use it for a short period of time. Then it will be up to them to decide whether it is better for them and to continue using it.

Since the Cornell Format will probably be a new concept to most of your students, you should first teach the complete process to them. Obviously, the next step is to have them actually use the format. You can have them transcribe notes from a previous lecture that they feel were taken poorly (See "Experiment with a Strategy from This Chapter") using this new format. You can lecture on new material and have them take notes using the Cornell Format. However, the most effective exercise is to have your students actually take notes in the new format in one of their other academic courses.

Remember that no matter which activity you choose, you should review the notes that the students have taken to ensure that they have taken this exercise seriously and that they are using the method correctly. Finally, have all of your students, including the "good" ones who believe that their notes are sufficient, use the new format to take notes in at least one lecture. As stated before, they will never know if there is something better available to them if they don't try something new.

Additional Activities and Exercises

Template To ensure that your students properly use the Cornell Format to take notes in several of their lectures, make a template of a blank note page that is properly divided and lined for the Cornell Format. Print copies of the template page, and distribute three or four copies to each student.

Experiment with a Strategy Note that the "Experiment with a Strategy from This Chapter" in the *Master Student Guide* provides an excellent introductory activity to the Cornell Format. This exercise asks students to rewrite their notes from a recent lecture using the Cornell Format. (See page 153 for complete instructions.) This will allow students to practice this new note-taking method before using it in an actual lecture.

Good or Bad After your students have used the Cornell Format to take notes in several lectures, conduct a class discussion that provides an opportunity for your students to give feedback about this new method. Ask your students what they liked and disliked about the method, the reasons for their views, any benefit they gained from the Cornell Format, and whether they would continue to use the method.

Study!!! Have your students select a course that they are presently taking in which to try using the Cornell Format. Have each student take notes using the format in all of the lectures leading up to the next exam in that class. They will then use these notes to study for the exam. After taking the exam and receiving their grade on it, have each student write a brief essay (one page or less) discussing their opinion of the Cornell Format and whether they gained any academic benefit from using it. If you are going to have your students attempt this exercise, remind them that they must still remember to focus on the content of the lecture, not only on the format of the note-taking. These will be the notes from which the student will study for his or her exam. Therefore, it is important to capture all of the necessary and relevant information.

Chapter 13: Notes: Experimenting with Maps

There are many different forms of note-taking. The Cornell Format is similar to traditional note-taking in structure. Some students, however, do not always think in highly structured ways. They often think and conceptualize abstractly and visually. Some students might prefer a technique that is less formal and uses less structure. Fortunately, they do not have to be restricted in their note-taking and studying. Chapter 13 introduces a less structured, more abstract method of taking notes: mapping.

Maps provide a more visual picture of notes than traditional methods do. They also may do a better job of showing relationships for some students. These mapping techniques might be of great benefit to those students who think abstractly, visually, or graphically and to those students who have difficulty with more traditional ideas of organization. Instead of forcing these students into formats that are not natural for them and with which they must struggle, mapping could provide a new, unique way to define concepts, show relationships, and link ideas that could allow students to maximize the potential of their notes.

This chapter will:

- introduce the concept of taking notes by building maps.
- explain the advantages of using maps to take notes.
- introduce two types of maps that are useful for note-taking: mind maps and concept maps.
- explain how to create a mind map when taking notes.
- provide ideas for the best ways to study from mind maps (see the sidebar on page 160).

- explain how to create concept maps when taking notes.
- provide ideas for the best ways to study from concept maps (see the sidebar on page 164).
- describe other ways to visually or graphically take notes.

Suggestions for Teaching

As mentioned in the discussion of Cornell Notes (Chapter 12), students can be resistant to change and trying new things. Since the concepts introduced in this chapter are less similar to their traditional ideas of note-taking, they may exhibit more resistance to the introduction of these mapping techniques. Be cognizant of this fact and ready for such resistance. Remind your students that they will never be able to take advantage of the potential benefits of new opportunities if they never try anything new. Also, you may want to point out that they are not required to use these methods of note-taking for their entire college careers. If they try them and do not find them useful, they can go back to some other method. Remember that not all students think visually in abstract concepts. Some students think textually in a highly organized structure. These students will struggle with mapping and quickly turn away from it. The objective of introducing these different note-taking methods is not to have students embrace all of them, but to make students aware of the many alternatives available to them and allow them to choose what they believe will work best for them.

As was the case with the Cornell Format (as you saw if you taught that method to your students), mapping will probably be a new concept to most of your students. Therefore, you should first teach each of the complete mapping techniques to them. Obviously, the next step is to have them actually use one or both of these mapping techniques. If you have enough time, I would recommend that you assign exercises to your students using each of the techniques. One of the main objectives of these chapters on note-taking is to expose your students to a variety of note-taking methods so they can choose the one that works best for them. Therefore, they should try out as many of the methods as possible.

You can have your students transcribe notes from a previous lecture that they feel were taken poorly (see "Experiment with a Strategy from This Chapter") using one or both mapping techniques. You can lecture on new material and have them take notes using mind maps, concept maps, or both methods. As with Cornell Notes, the most effective exercise is to have your students take notes in one of their other academic courses using one or both mapping techniques.

Remember that no matter which activity you choose, you should review the notes that the students have taken to ensure that they have taken this exercise seriously and that they are using the method correctly. Finally, have all of your students, including the "good" ones who believe that their notes are sufficient, use a new technique to take notes in at least one lecture. Encourage them as well to compare notes with one another and with students in their other courses, so they can share ideas on the best methods to use. Emphasize the benefit of experimentation as they seek to find the best method for themselves. As stated before, they will never know if there is something better available to them if they don't try something new.

Additional Activities and Exercises

Map the News Have your students watch a broadcast of the evening news and take brief notes. During the commercial breaks or directly after the news broadcast, each student should create a mind map from these notes. Students should bring the maps to the next class to discuss or submit.

Colors Have each student take one of the mind maps that he or she has created and experiment with adding color to it. They can use color to represent or link any topics, categories, relationships, and the like. For the purpose of this exercise, students should make their mind maps as colorful as possible.

Study!!! Have your students select a course that they are presently taking and in which they will take notes using either mind or concept mapping. Have each student take notes using the chosen method in all of the lectures leading up to the next exam in that class. They will then use these notes to study for the exam. After taking the exam and receiving their grade on it, have each student write a brief essay (one page or less) discussing their opinions of the Cornell Format and whether they gained any academic benefit from using it. If you are going to have your students attempt this exercise, remind them that they must still remember to focus on the content of the lecture, not only on the format of the note-taking. These will be the notes from which the student will study for his or her exam. Therefore, it is important to capture all of the necessary and relevant information.

Good or Bad After your students have used mind and concept mapping to take notes in several lectures, conduct a class discussion that provides an opportunity for your students to give feedback about these new methods. Ask your students what they liked and disliked about each method, the reasons for their views, any benefit they gained from them, and whether they would continue to use either of them. If you are teaching an online course, this discussion may be particularly helpful since you may not have the option of actually viewing their notes.

Cornell Mind Map Have your students combine the techniques of mind mapping with the Cornell Format. Have your students take notes in their next lecture using the Cornell Format. They should only fill in the right-hand side of their Cornell sheets. Then they should bring these notes to your next class. Have each student create mind maps of the notes in the cue columns of their Cornell sheets.

The Big Mind Map Conduct a short lecture on the next topic from your syllabus. Divide the students in your class into small groups. Provide each group with a large piece of poster paper and markers. Have each group use the notes that they have taken from this lecture and create a large mind map. Have each group present its mind map to the class.

Graphic Notes by Groups Conduct a short lecture on the next topic from your syllabus. Divide the students in your class into small groups. Assign each group a different type of graphic note-taking method to use to construct a "note map." For example, assign a concept map, a timeline, and a comparison chart to different groups. (Note: You will have to structure the lecture that you give to accommodate information that can be used in these more selective formats.)

Chapter 14: Notes: Experimenting with Outlines

It is possible that your students might have had negative experiences with outlining in the past. When writing and preparing reports, teachers often require students to use rigid outline formats based on Roman numerals and other combinations of letters and numbers. This style, however, represents only one outlining format. If students can approach outlining in a more open and flexible way and experiment with other formats, they can discover the power of outlining to reveal relationships between ideas and to categorize and organize large amounts of information.

Outlining also can be an advantage when a student encounters material that is presented in a disorganized way. Remember that it is inevitable that every student will face such a disorganized presentation of information at some point. Outlining can give students an effective method for overcoming this challenge, instead of surrendering to frustration and less than effective study from poorly taken notes that are difficult to decipher.

This chapter will:

- introduce the concept of outlining as an effective method of note-taking.
- explain the advantages of taking notes using outlining.

- teach students how to create outlines when taking notes.
- identify and describe different types of outlines that can be used in note-taking.
- explain how to use a computer to create outlines.
- provide ideas for the best ways to study from outlines.

Suggestions for Teaching

As has been said throughout this section on note-taking, students can be resistant to change. Their first reaction to the concepts presented in this chapter might be either an expression of dislike for outlining or the feeling that outlining is only used when writing papers. However, if your students are open to the possibilities of outlining, they might discover a powerful new tool in their arsenal of study techniques. After all, the objective of introducing these different note-taking methods is not to have students embrace all of them, but to make students aware of the many alternatives available to them and allow them to choose what they believe will work best for them.

As was the case with the note-taking techniques that were presented in previous chapters (and as you are aware if you taught any or all of those methods to your students) outlining as a method of note-taking might be a new concept to many of your students. Therefore, you should first teach the complete process of outlining to them. Obviously, the next step is to have your students use outlining to take notes on a lecture or chapter in one of their textbooks.

As explained in the previous chapters, you can have your students transcribe notes from a previous lecture that they feel were taken poorly (see "Experiment with a Strategy from This Chapter") using an outlining method. You can lecture on new material and have them outline to take notes. However, the most effective exercise is to have your students take notes in one of their other academic courses using an outlining technique.

Remember that no matter which activity you choose, you should review the notes that the students have taken to ensure that they have taken this exercise seriously and that they are using the method correctly. Finally, have all of your students, including the "good" ones who believe that their notes are sufficient, use some form of outlining to take notes in at least one lecture. As stated before, they will never know if there is something better available to them if they don't try something new.

Additional Activities and Exercises

Outline the News Have your students watch a broadcast of the evening news and take brief notes. Directly after the news broadcast, each student should create an outline from these notes. Students should bring the outlines to the next class meeting to discuss or submit.

Outlining TV This is a variation of the preceding "Outline the News" activity. Have each student select a popular comedy or dramatic television program to watch. The chosen program should be at least one half-hour long. Students should take brief notes while watching the program. Immediately after the television show ends, each student should create an outline from these notes. Students should bring the outlines to the next class meeting to discuss or submit.

Study!!! Have your students select a course that they are presently taking and in which they will take notes using one of the outlining methods discussed in Chapter 14. Have each student take notes using the chosen method in all of the lectures leading up to the next exam in that class. They will then use these notes to study for the exam. After taking the exam and receiving their grade on it, have each student write a brief essay (one page or less) discussing their opinions of outlining as a note-taking tool and whether they gained any academic benefit from using it. If you are going to have your students attempt this exercise, remind them that they must still remember to focus on the content of the lecture, not only on the format of the note-taking. These will be the notes from which the student will study for his or her exam. Therefore, it is important to capture all of the necessary and relevant information.

Topics versus Sentences Have each student bring the notes they have taken during a recent lecture to your class. Students should rewrite their notes in a topic outline format. Next, they should rewrite the same notes in a sentence outline format. Conduct a classroom discussion that compares and contrasts the two outlining methods. (Be sure to focus on the ease of study offered by the first method and the easy conversion of the outline into an essay offered by the latter.)

Computer Outlines Conduct a short lesson on the creation of outlines using a word processing program such as Microsoft Word. Have your students practice outlining on the computer using the features that you have taught.

Chapter 15: Creating More Value from Your Notes

As stated in the *Master Student Guide for Academic Success*, the purpose of taking notes is to consult them later. To some students, that means looking them over only once or twice before a test. However, a significant amount of time may have passed between the class in which the notes were taken and the day that they will be used for study. By that time these old notes may raise more questions than they answer, causing difficulty in studying and maybe even becoming useless.

After spending time learning how to take notes that are well organized and meaningful, it is important that these notes are now used to their fullest potential. They should not be left for a single review before a test, but they can and should be used throughout a semester. Students can do this by updating, condensing, reorganizing, reviewing, refining, and using them to predict test questions. By following these steps, students can add much greater value to their notes.

Students should not merely take notes, put them away, and then review them several times immediately before an exam. Notes should become an active, useful tool for learning. Chapter 15 develops steps to teach students to prepare and use their notes in such a way.

This chapter will:

- explain how students should view and use their notes in order to gain maximum value from them.
- teach students how to revise their notes.
- provide guidelines that students can use to evaluate the quality and focus of their notes (see sidebar on page 173).
- develop schedules to use to review notes in a timely manner.
- suggest the use of a personal academic journal to enhance the understanding of course material.
- describe the focus and methodology to be used in the academic journal just described.
- identify the two types of notes that can be taken by students when reading.

Suggestions for Teaching

The first challenge that you will encounter will be to convince your students of the benefits to be gained if they actively use their notes throughout a semester. Your initial lecture can detail the difficulties and disadvantages of trying to memorize and learn many weeks of material in one or two nights. Continue on to explain that college coursework often requires a deeper level of understanding and analysis than simple memorization. In one session it is often difficult to memorize large amounts of information, transform this information into more intellectual concepts, comprehend these concepts and theories, and develop all of this into potential test questions from which to prepare for an exam. Therefore, it is most beneficial for students to prepare and interact with their notes from the time that they are first taken through the weeks up to the exam that covers the material for which those notes were taken.

As you detail the increased value that can be built into and gained from the active use of students' notes and explain the various methods by which this can be accomplished, your students will listen politely. Some students will agree with you. Many will be unconvinced or simply not want to bother to spend the time prior to their exams. The ultimate proof is in actually doing something. Therefore, the best way to convince your students of the value and benefit of the methods in this chapter is to have your students try them out. If students use them and comprehend the material more easily, spend less stressful time studying immediately preceding an exam, and earn an equivalent or higher test grade (than they usually do), they will be more likely to adopt the methods that you have taught them.

Toward these ends, have each of your students pick a course in which they will use their notes up to the time of their next exam according to your directions. The ideal situation is one in which your students all take a common course. (This lesson will obviously extend two to six weeks after its initial introduction. You may want to check your students' notes and their progress at least once a week to make sure that they are actually using the methods that you have taught them.) Review the steps for revising, condensing, updating, and writing test questions. Have each student set up a weekly or daily schedule of review and work to be done with their notes. Use this procedure for one complete testing cycle, that is, from the first day that new material is presented for an exam up to the actual taking of the exam. When the exams are returned, have your students discuss how they felt about the process, its advantages and disadvantages, if they earned a higher grade than on previous exams, and if they think that they will use the same methods again in the future.

Chapter 15 also introduces another new concept whose benefit you will probably also have to convince your students of. The chapter suggests the use of a journal to enhance the value of notes and increase the understanding of complex material. Your students will probably not rush to embrace additional work in the form of journal writing to support note-taking, especially your adult learners, students with full- or part-time jobs or family obligations, or student athletes who have practice and games, in addition to their course work. If you choose to introduce this topic, then you should explain that much college-level work requires the deep understanding of a subject, as well as the analysis of complex relationships, creativity, and the generation of unique thinking and ideas. The purpose of the academic journal described in this chapter is to enhance and supplement the work done through note-taking. The journal allows students to use a format through which they can think broadly and stretch out mentally. They can reflect on the significance of courses and the work that they have done, relate personal experiences and examples to the work, and proceed with less formality and structure toward a deeper comprehension and understanding of the course material. Finally, if you cover the topic of academic journal writing, then have each student select one of his or her courses and assign several journal-writing exercises to them.

Additional Activities and Exercises

Note Review Schedule Each student should develop a weekly schedule of review for the notes that he or she takes in each of his or her courses. Students should submit their final schedule to the instructor for comment and approval. When the schedule has been approved, the times of study and review should be transferred into the student's daily or weekly planner.

Revise Your Notes Have each student bring in notes that he or she has taken during several recent lectures. Each student should clean them up (i.e., fix passages that are illegible, write out abbreviations, expand on hard-to-understand sections, etc.) and/or neatly recreate them in a new format. Review each student's notes to ensure that they are neat, clear, and well organized.

Partner Review Have each student bring in notes that he or she has taken during a recent lecture in your course or in one of his or her other courses. The notes may or may not have been cleaned up and revised prior to this activity. Divide the class into pairs of students. Have the first student in each pair review his or her notes out loud to his or her partner. The partner will then critique the usefulness of the notes in studying for an upcoming exam. Reverse roles and repeat the process. This may work particularly well in a learning community or major-specific course, where common academic material can be used.

Academic Journal I Have each student keep an academic journal for one month to one semester. Entries should be made in the journal at least twice per week. The entries should relate to the work that they are covering in their college courses. It should consist of questions about difficult material; reflections on concepts, theories, ideas, and opinions; observations on relationships between concepts; feelings about how course material relates to student's lives and the larger world; and so on.

Academic Journal II Have each student keep an academic journal for one month to one semester. The purpose of these journal entries will be to help students deal with stress, course and test anxiety, and self-doubt. Students should work through these feelings by writing about them whenever they occur. Students should acknowledge these feelings by writing them down in a journal entry. They should also try to determine what is causing the anxiety, stress, confusion, doubt, and so on, and why they feel that way. Finally, each entry should contain some action that the student will take to deal with or overcome this obstacle.

Exam Questions Have each student review his or her notes from several recent lectures. From these notes, students should create a list of questions that they believe will appear on the next exam. If your students attend a common core course or are part of a learning community, combine the lists of all students into a single comprehensive list. Distribute this final list to your students so that they can use it to study for their next exam. Consider conducting a study session in one of your classes using this large list.

Building Memory and Test-Taking Skills

Chapter 16: Memory: Storing Ideas and Information

As Chapter 16 points out, memory is a process. That is, it is a series of strategies that we use to create mental representations of past events. A memory appears as a discrete mental event--an image, a series of words, a smell, or some other form that we recall. In learning, we are most concerned with the process of *recalling* that stored image, definition, theory, or whatever piece of information that has been put into our minds. However, how well one recalls the image, definition, and so on is also dependent on how well one initially creates the memory. Therefore, in the *Master Student Guide*, the topic of memory will be broken down into two dependent parts or processes – creation and retrieval.

The art of improving memory can be defined as increasing the probability of being able to retrieve stored information when we want it. In other words, how do we put it in there so that we are most likely to be able to get it out when we want and need it? This chapter (16) focuses on putting it in (creation) – storing information, images, events, data in the best and most efficient way. The next chapter (17) addresses getting it out (retrieval).

This chapter will:

- develop a brief explanation of the process of memory.
- introduce ways to set the stage to remember.
- provide a checklist of quick ways to relax (see checklist "Sixty Seconds to Relaxation" on page 186).
- explain the three stages of memory: sensory, short-term, and long-term memory.
- explain the process of elaboration.
- develop and explain a list of methods to enhance and increase elaboration.
- introduce five ways to organize large groups of information (see sidebar on page 192).
- introduce the seven "R's" of remembering (see checklist on page 193).

Suggestions for Teaching

Many students simply believe that they either have a good memory or they don't. They do not necessarily perceive this area as being one of the skills that they can meaningfully develop. Some students who may have been away from higher education for many years might believe that their powers of memorization and recall have faded significantly.

One of your first tasks might be to explain the processes of memory and memorization so that your students understand that there are strategies to improve and maximize the effectiveness of memory. You could begin by separating memory into two related stages, creation and retrieval, and explain the relationship between them. It is important for students to understand that although it is vital for them to be able to get the right fact or concept at the right time (for classroom discussion or for an exam), this strategic retrieval is often dependent upon how well the facts were put into their minds in the first place. Therefore, the remainder of this chapter will focus on this creation or input process.

First, explain how to set the stage to remember. Discuss relaxation, reduction of distractions, environment, focus, a positive attitude, and a schedule of learning or review. This topic provides an excellent opportunity for students to practice mild relaxation and controlled breathing techniques. Students will often agree that ideas such as these are good ones, but they will not actively adopt them. The best way to convince students of the techniques' great benefit and to encourage the more likely use of them is to actually demonstrate them. Doing so can also provide a welcome and enjoyable diversion from the normal routine of class.

The next topic addressed in the chapter is elaboration or the encoding of information. This is the key process of moving information from short-term to long-term memory where it will need to stay until the student requires it at some future time. The *Master Student Guide* develops many strategies, such as associations, mnemonics, categorizations, recitation, and the like, to enhance this vital step.

As with most other topics, you should assign exercises to your students where they actually use the methods that you have taught. Give them a set of new facts and have them arrange the facts using a mnemonic system, for example. Or, better yet, have your students bring to class their notes from a lecture in one of their other subjects and use one of these new strategies to memorize several pages of notes. Note when the next exam is for the chosen class. After the exam has been taken, have your students evaluate whether their new strategies helped them recall the notes for which they were used.

Finally, I would suggest that you take some time to emphasize the very important, but often overlooked, topic of repetition and over preparation. Many students study with the objective of spending just enough time to learn whatever material there is for an exam. But this becomes self-defeating, since the student does not know exactly what information will be on the exam until he or she actually takes the exam.

The objective should be to find a way to study and remember all of the information that *could* be on the exam. In this way, a student is prepared to recall any information from any potential source that might find its way onto the exam. In other words, a student should know all of the *possible* information so that she can answer any potential question on the test. She should be over prepared. This is the true path to great academic success. And by using the techniques developed in Chapters 16 and 17, it is not as difficult as one might think.

Additional Activities and Exercises

Distraction Discussion Divide your class into small groups. Each group should create a list of all of the things that distract the group members when they read, study, focus on schoolwork, and so on. Each group will present its list to the class in order to create one large list. The class will then discuss each distraction and develop a way in which to eliminate, overcome, or avoid it.

Mnemonics Divide your class into pairs of students. Distribute groups of words, objects, topics, and the like that the students will use to develop mnemonic sentences. For example, a list of animals could be a lion, tiger, bear, rabbit, snake, eagle, whale, and albatross. Or a list of presidents could be Lincoln, Reagan, Bush, Washington, Kennedy, Hoover, and Jefferson. Each student must develop a mnemonic sentence to represent the items on the list. In other words, the first letter of a word in the sentence is the first letter of an item in the group. The class members will vote on which sentence is the silliest. You may want to even award a prize for the silliest sentence.

Visual Pictures This activity is a variation of the mnemonic activity. Divide the class into pairs of students. Distribute several lists of words, objects, topics, and so on. Each student should develop a single visual picture that includes all of the items in the group. The class members will vote on the silliest image that was created.

Memory Evaluation Have each student choose several memory techniques, such as visual pictures, relaxation, repetition, mnemonics, that he or she will use to study for an upcoming exam. After the students have studied and taken their exams, have them write a short essay or journal entry describing the methods that they used, whether they enjoyed the methods, whether the methods helped them achieve a high grade on the exam, and why or why not the methods helped.

Remember Your Keys Have each student select something that he or she often forgets, such as car keys. Have each student write a short essay describing the item that he or she frequently forgets, as well as at least one strategy that he or she will use to remember that item in the future.

Seven R's Divide the students in your class into pairs. Give each member of a pair a different set of items to memorize. Have the first member go through each of the seven steps of remembering in the checklist on page 193 of Chapter 16 in the *Master Student Guide.* The first student should go through all seven steps once. Then have the other partner complete the seven steps using his or her own list of items. After each partner has memorized his or her list using the seven steps, each student will attempt to recite his or her list from memory. Repeat the exercise until all items have been memorized. You can distribute additional lists and have the students repeat the activity until they can memorize a list in a single turn through the seven steps.

Chapter 17: Memory: Recalling Ideas and Information

Sometimes it seems as if a student's entire academic life is comprised of recalling facts and information that have been previously stored away. Although this description is not completely accurate (much time is spent solving problems and thinking creatively, after all), a large part of a student's grade *is* the result of giving information back to her professor. And that information must be exactly what the professor is looking for. In other words, it must be the "correct" information or the "right" answer according to the professor, not what the student might think is the "right" answer.

Hopefully, students will have learned how to encode information accurately, or put the right things into memory, by using the methods that were introduced and explained in Chapter 16. Some length of time will have surely elapsed, however, before students are called upon to retrieve that information and use it or present it to the professor. How can students improve the likelihood that they will be able to recall accurately the information that was put in some time ago? Chapter 17 addresses this challenge and provides methods and strategies to increase the probability of successful information retrieval and thereby enhance academic success.

This chapter will:

- explain memory in terms of encoding, storing, and retrieving.
- explain the importance of relaxation and focus.
- introduce and explain common information-retrieval techniques.
- introduce the concept of recreating original context to aid retrieval.
- reinforce the importance of repetition and review.
- remind students of the importance of sleep to keen mental awareness.

Suggestions for Teaching

Since Chapters 16 and 17 are linked together, your students already should be convinced of the importance of accurate memory input and the recovery of the exact information that was previously stored in memory. Therefore, you can focus on the factors and techniques that promote successful information retrieval.

Point out to your students that stress can be a major obstacle to accurate memory recall. Students can often feel that there is so much to remember and that it is so important to be able to come up with the right answers when faced with exam questions or confronted by the prospect of having to answer questions in class that they create high levels of tension and anxiety for themselves. Of course, the anxiety and stress then become major obstacles to the retrieval process. Often, students create situations for themselves in which they are able to remember very little.

It is important for you to help your students confront such anxiety. Teach them to focus and to relax. This chapter presents several effective relaxation techniques. Review them with your students and consider practicing them in class. Scores earned on exams make up a significant part of a student's course grade, and low exam scores that are earned as a result of poor memory recall due to test anxiety can negatively impact a student's academic success, as well as his self-esteem. Although it may appear to be less of an academic topic, learning how to relax in the face of tension and stress is time well spent.

Next, consider teaching your students the importance of focusing on the task that confronts them. Students are very busy, and many things compete for their attention. Job responsibilities, social obligations, parents, child-care issues, roommate problems, grocery shopping, laundry, athletic competitions, and relationship issues, among many other things, can all compete for a student's attention and distract him or her from the task at hand. Teach your students how to actively block distractions from their minds for short periods of time and focus clearly on one thing – the chemistry exam, for example. If you are teaching this chapter as part of your academic course, take a few minutes before your next exam and practice several relaxation techniques with your students and actively focus them on the test material.

In addition to the most common memory retrieval techniques that are outlined in Chapter 17, there are several topics that might be less familiar but can merit special attention. For example, when a student cannot remember the information that she is searching for, an excellent strategy is to recreate the context in which the information was originally encoded. That is, have the student remember being in the original place in which she studied the information. If she studied in the library, she should picture herself at the desk at which she studied with her books and notes spread out before her, sitting cross-legged with a pencil in her mouth reviewing her notes. Putting herself back into this situation often allows her to go back into her memory and pull out the facts that she was searching for.

Also of great importance is old-fashioned repetition and review. Repeating facts often helps keep them fresh in one's memory. A well-planned schedule of review is much more beneficial than one long session of study the night before an exam. As stated at the end of the last section, there is no better strategy than over preparation to ensure academic success. Also, remind your students of the importance of getting enough sleep. Whether one is an athlete or a student, one cannot perform at one's best if one's mind and body is not well rested. Sleep is often the easiest thing to cut back on when faced with a very hectic schedule, but lack of sleep can produce several negative consequences that many people and students are not aware of.

Finally, remind students not to get discouraged and not to give up when they cannot immediately recall the facts or information that they want. Do not panic. Do not create stress and anxiety, but simply move on to the next question or quietly clear one's mind. Often some time away from the question allows the answer to flow up to one's realization (memory) and allows one to retrieve the information that is needed to answer the question correctly.

Additional Activities and Exercises

Distraction-Free Zone Divide your class into small groups. Have each group discuss the distractions that they encounter when they study. Then have each group create a distraction-free zone. That is, they should develop an image of the perfect study environment that will be free of all interruptions, disturbances, and distractions. Each group should present its description of the distraction-free zone to the class.

The Body Scan In order to practice relieving stress, have your students perform the checklist on page 196 of Chapter 17 ("Relax with a Body Scan"). Have students lie on the floor with an arm or book under their heads. If you prepare your students ahead of time, you can have them bring a small pillow into class. Students close their eyes and rest their attention on the soles of their feet. Notice and release any tension in that part of the body. Use the same "notice and release" techniques as students slowly move their attention through their calves, knees, thighs, pelvis, stomach, chest, shoulders, arms, neck, and head. After successfully completing this exercise, have your students take their seats. Students should repeat the exercise at their seats so that they feel comfortable performing it when they encounter stress in a classroom situation.

Stress Relief Have your students perform the breathing exercises in the checklist found on page 186 in Chapter 16, "Sixty Seconds to Relaxation."

Context Memory Have each student pick a subject to study. The night before your class each student should study notes from that chosen class. Students should bring those notes to your class. Divide the class into pairs of students. The first student should quiz his or her partner on the notes that he or she studied the previous evening. Whenever the student cannot remember an answer, he or she should describe the context in which he or she studied the night before. In other words, he or she should begin by describing the location, the room, the time, the order of material studied, and so on. Students are practicing the recreation of the context in which the memory was created in order to help stimulate the retrieval of the desired information. When the first student's notes are completed, the partners should switch roles.

Anxiety and Stress Conduct a class discussion on the ways that stress and anxiety can interfere with a student's study session and block memory recall. Develop methods to deal with and reduce stress in these situations.

I Can't Remember the Answer!! At times, most students have found themselves in a situation where they cannot remember information that they have studied and that they knew the night before. Conduct a class discussion about the tricks and methods that can be used to overcome this temporary memory lapse and reclaim this temporarily lost answer.

Sleep Discussion Conduct a class discussion about the importance of getting enough sleep each night. How do you know what the right amount of sleep is for you? What are the common obstacles to getting the proper amount of sleep? Have your students develop ways to ensure that they can get at least eight hours of sleep each night.

Review It Have each student set up a formal schedule of review of their notes leading up to the next exam in your class or one of their other courses. At minimum, the schedule will include a review of new notes within twenty-four hours; brief, regular review of all notes at least twice per week; and two study sessions immediately preceding the exam for which they are preparing. Make sure that your students stick to this schedule. Have each student submit a short essay evaluating the effectiveness of this study schedule after they have taken the exam.

Chapter 18: Preparing for Tests

At almost every college in the United States, it is inevitable that at some point every student must face taking exams in most of his or her courses. Often, scores earned on exams contribute the largest share of the total grade that a student earns in a course. Therefore, it is extremely important to master the skills needed to take tests successfully.

The act of taking a test is not merely sitting down and answering questions but, in fact, consists of two distinct parts. The first is preparation, which is the focus of this chapter. The second (which is addressed in Chapter 19) are the strategies used to complete an exam successfully and earn the highest possible score on that exam. Each of these events is separate but related to the other, and by mastering the skills of both a student can work to maximize his academic success.

This chapter will:

- explain the benefits of extensive test preparation.
- introduce and describe effective test preparation strategies.
- describe how to prepare and organize notes and other materials for review.
- explain the advantages of creating mock questions/tests to enhance study effectiveness and test performance.
- explain how to create a schedule of regular review.
- describe the advantages of study groups.
- address the issue of test anxiety and provide strategies to deal with the problem.
- provide a checklist of things to do before a test (see checklist on page 213).

Suggestions for Teaching

When a student thinks about preparing to take a test, the first thing that comes to mind is probably reviewing his or her notes. But the notes themselves provide only a starting point for test preparation.

In fact, untouched notes are only raw material for the process. As was first described in Chapters 11 and 15, after notes have been taken initially, they should be reworked into some format that provides maximum benefit in their review and study. Here again, as instructor, you want to make sure that your students feel comfortable manipulating, rearranging, and reorganizing their notes into a format that best facilitates effective test preparation. Notes are not carved into stone; rather they are like clay waiting to be shaped into whatever form provides the most value to a student's study time.

But what is the best format to provide the most value for study? That depends on the purpose for which they will be used. So if notes are the raw material of test preparation, the first step in the process is to step back and define the purpose for which they will be used. Notes are used to learn the material that will appear on an exam. It is not an end in itself, however, to simply learn all of the material. One must be able to use that material to provide the correct answers to the questions that the professor is asking on the exam. Providing these correct answers in turn should earn a student a high score on the test. So notes are used for two purposes: to learn the material and earn a high test score.

A student should begin by trying to determine what material will be on a test and how the questions might be asked to assess his or her knowledge of that material. In other words, students should try to work backward in order to maximize study efficiency. As much as it is possible, students should try to figure out how the test and the questions will be structured on an exam and then organize their notes to answer these questions. This helps to maximize the efficiency of study time by directing students first to the material that is most likely to be on an exam and then to spend more time on this material. Although it is beneficial to study all the information that might possibly be covered, this is not always possible. And not all material is of equal importance, so this method forces prioritization and organization.

In addition, this strategy helps memory recall, which is another important aspect of taking tests successfully (see Chapter 17). By anticipating questions that might appear on an exam and developing answers to these questions while studying, it aids memory and helps create a context in which recall might be easier. As a result, your students can gain great benefit in their exam scores by working backward from the anticipated test to their notes in this way.

In addition to the strategy just described, Chapter 18 provides many excellent ideas that students can use to prepare for an exam. Choose any or all of them to review. They all provide great benefit to your students. In particular, be sure to point out the benefits gained by regularly reviewing material well in advance of the actual test date. In fact, students can actually create a weekly review schedule based upon the methods explained in the chapter.

Also remind your students of the importance of solving the problems and performing the calculations that they believe will appear on a test. There is no substitute for this practice, and it is always best to do many of these problems before a test. It also helps to prepare students for the many variations of a single type of problem that they might encounter.

The chapter also addresses the many benefits of study groups. Many students do not take advantage of this effective study strategy, preferring to study only by themselves. As a result, you might choose to spend some time discussing the many advantages of this strategy and suggest ways to best utilize the strengths and support of others for test preparation.

Finally, Chapter 18 concludes with the topic of test anxiety. Do not underestimate the size of this obstacle, even if students will not always acknowledge it. Therefore, it is beneficial to conduct a lesson on ways to reduce test anxiety. The chapter offers many strategies students can take advantage of for their test preparation. And, of course, the realization that one is fully prepared can help to lessen feelings of anxiety and panic when one is confronted by a blank test.

Of course, it may be helpful to assign activities and exercises to help your students practice these skills and strategies. You can create activities that use any of the skills in the chapter (or see the suggestions at the end of this chapter). However, you can provide the most benefit to your students by using an exam in your course (if you are teaching this chapter as part of an academic course) or by having your students prepare for an actual exam in one of their academic core courses. That is, spend one or two class sessions reorganizing notes and using many of the techniques explained in the chapter. Organize and prepare your students' study sessions for an upcoming exam. Then have them study accordingly. After your students take their exams, you can discuss their results and how they felt about the various methods that they tried. Although more time consuming than shorter class activities, this approach will provide the most value to your students' portfolios of academic skills.

Additional Activities and Exercises

Study Checklist Have each student create a study checklist for their upcoming exams in each of their courses. Do not confuse this checklist with a review schedule for notes. Neither is it a review sheet. It is a list of all activities that must be completed in preparation for an exam, including textbook pages to be read, special articles that must be read, note review, problems to be completed, and so on. See page 204 in Chapter 18 for an excellent example of a study checklist. Review each student's checklist once a week to ensure that they are completing activities as scheduled.

The Body Scan In order to practice relieving stress, have your students perform the checklist on page 196 of Chapter 17 ("Relax with a Body Scan"). Have students lie on the floor with an arm or book under their heads. If you prepare your students ahead of time, you can have them bring a small pillow into class. Students close their eyes and rest their attention on the soles of their feet. Notice and release any tension in that part of the body. Use the same "notice and release" techniques as students slowly move their attention through their calves, knees, thighs, pelvis, stomach, chest, shoulders, arms, neck, and head. After successfully completing this exercise, have your students take their seats. Students should repeat the exercise at their seats so that they feel comfortable performing it when they encounter stress in a classroom situation.

Stress Relief Have your students perform the breathing exercises in the checklist found on page 186 in Chapter 16, "Sixty Seconds to Relaxation."

Review It Have each student set up a formal schedule for reviewing their notes leading up to the next exam in your class or one of their other courses. At a minimum, the schedule will include a review of new notes within twenty-four hours; brief, regular review of all notes at least twice per week; and two study sessions immediately preceding the exam for which they are preparing. Make sure that your students stick to this schedule. Have each student submit a short essay evaluating the effectiveness of this study schedule after they have taken the exam.

Summary Notes Have each student identify the course in which he or she will have his or her next exam. Students should bring in their notes for the material for this exam several days before the scheduled time to take this exam. Each student should create summary notes to use for study for this exam. That is, they should rewrite their notes, condensing and organizing them into several concise pages from which they will study for the exam. Check each student's summary notes upon completion of this exercise.

Exam Questions Have each student bring in notes from the last several sessions of one of his or her classes. Or, use the notes that your students have taken from the last several lectures that you have given. From these notes, have each student develop a list of test questions that he or she believes the instructor might ask on the next exam.

Group Exam Questions Have each student review his or her notes from several recent lectures. From these notes, students should create a list of questions that they believe will appear on the next exam. If your students attend a common core course or are part of a learning community, combine the lists of all students into a single comprehensive list. Distribute this final list to your students so they can use it to study for their next exam. Consider conducting a study session in one of your classes using this large list.

Study Groups Have your students form study groups made up of three to four students per group. The groups should consist of students who are all taking the same course. The students will conduct one or two study sessions in which the members will study together for the next exam in the course that they have identified. After all groups have taken their exams, each group will report the results of and their opinions about the study sessions to the class.

Twenty Things I Like One way to relieve tension is to stop what one is doing and substitute a pleasant image for one's stressful thoughts and emotions. The purpose of this activity is to create a supply of pleasant thoughts and images to recall during a time of stress. Have each student conduct an eight-minute brainstorm to generate at least twenty things that he or she likes to do. When the list is completed, study it and pick out two or three activities that seem especially pleasant. Elaborate on them and write down all of the memories that you have about them. Use these images to regain calm in stressful situations, such as exams.

Exaggerate Your Fear Divide the class into small groups. Have each group take ten minutes to come up with the most outrageous and worst thing that will happen to them if they fail an exam. At the end of the exercise, have each group present its results to the class. Award a prize for the most outrageous result.

Practice a Test Develop a practice test for the students in your class. This test can be a general-knowledge test or a test of silly questions. Or use one of the old exams from your class. The test should include a variety of different types of questions, such as true/false, multiple-choice, short-answer, and so on. Have your students take the exam. Review the results with the entire class. Use the review as a way to discuss the best methods to be used when answering the different types of questions.

Chapter 19: Using Test Time Efficiently

Taking a test is different than studying for a test. Students do not face time constraints while studying for an exam, other than those that they artificially place on themselves. If a student does not know the answer when studying, she can always go back to check her notes. Most exams, however, must be completed within a specific amount of time, and few testing situations allow students to check their notes to find the correct answers.

In addition to the constraints imposed by these conditions, test-taking situations can create anxiety and even panic for many students, even for those who are academically successful. Also, don't forget that some of your students are returning to school after a long time away from the classroom, and they may not have taken a test for many years. They may find such a situation particularly stressful. This does not need to be the case, however.

Test conditions are often predictable, and, therefore, students can work to anticipate and prepare for them. Sufficient preparation can do much to alleviate anxiety, stress, and panic. Building on a student's successful preparation and review prior to taking a test (see Chapter 18), this chapter introduces many strategies that students can use to help them to succeed on any type of exam.

This chapter will:

- explain the differences between studying for a test and taking a test.
- teach students how to develop a test-taking plan.
- teach students how to budget their time when taking a test.
- discuss common test-taking errors and ways to avoid them.
- provide a checklist of things to do when a student gets stuck on a question (see checklist on page 218).
- provide specific test-taking strategies for true/false, multiple-choice, and essay exams.
- provide guidelines to use when making an educated guess to answer a test question (see checklist on page 220).

Suggestions for Teaching

Many students prepare to take an exam by studying. Some who prepare do so poorly, and a few take tests without studying at all (which is not recommended). Many students, however, have no strategy at all with which to take a test (which is also a mistake). This is your opportunity to teach them the great benefit that results from taking an exam with a carefully planned strategy that one begins to develop before even sitting down to take the test. As you have seen in Chapter 19, the *Master Student Guide* offers dozens of suggestions and skills to help students better navigate their way through taking all kinds of tests.

Perhaps the most important skill discussed in this chapter is the development of a test- taking plan. Many students simply sit down to take an exam and answer the questions as they come. This is not the best way to take a test. They should first find out as much information as they can about the structure of the test, what will be on the exam, and what is expected of them. The most obvious person from whom to obtain this information is the professor. Students should simply ask. Which is not to say that the professor will always answer all of their questions. But they will not know if they don't try. Next, students should match their study strategy to what they believe the structure of the test will be. And finally, they should develop a specific plan by which they will take the test. For example, they might review the exam as soon as it is handed out, write down any formulas or definitions that they see they will need later, evaluate the breakdown of points by question type, budget time, decide which questions to answer first, and so on. All of these suggestions are obvious, but, as you know, many students do not approach tests in this way.

I would like to point out several key areas that can yield great academic value for students. However, because they are obvious and simple I believe that they are sometimes forgotten or covered very quickly. Remind your students that in most cases they are permitted to write down key definitions, terms, concepts, or formulas (from memory). Students should write these items down in the margin of the test or on the back of one of the pages as soon as they sit down, especially the ones that they have had trouble recalling while studying. The exam is testing whether you have learned and can recall certain pieces of information (among other things). It does not matter if you write them down at the very beginning of the exam or an hour into the test. So, students should develop the habit of writing down the most important information or concepts that are most difficult to remember as soon as they begin their tests.

Students often ask for open-book tests. They believe that these exams provide an opportunity to earn a high grade because they are easier than closed-book exams. Point out that open-book tests are usually longer and require a much greater level of detail in their answers. Perhaps the time needed to prepare for them is less because they require less memorization, but they are often longer and more difficult to complete. Therefore, open-book exams usually offer little real advantage over those of the closed-book type.

Finally, remind your students to answer all the questions on the exam. I have always had at least one student who leaves one or more questions blank on every exam that I have ever given. I tell them to put something down even if they have no idea what the answer is. I tell them to write me a little story if all else fails. I had one student who would draw cartoons for me when he didn't know the answer. They were usually funny, and I would give him two or three points (out of ten). The point is that if a student leaves a question blank, he earns no points for that question. No matter what. No matter how generous you would like to be, you cannot award any points for an empty space. At least if he fills up that empty space with some answer, he has the opportunity to earn some points. And a few points are better than no points. Even more importantly, the simple act of writing (something) might eventually lead the student to recall the correct answer (see Chapter 17). Always try!

Additional Activities and Exercises

Favorite Tests Divide the class into groups. Have each group member contribute his or her favorite or preferred test-taking strategies. For example, strategies include answering all of the easy questions first or budgeting time by scanning the questions and allocating the estimated time needed to answer each one. Have one member compile all of the strategies into a single list. Have each group share its strategies with the class.

The Body Scan In order to practice relieving stress, have your students perform the checklist on page 196 of Chapter 17 ("Relax with a Body Scan"). Have students lie on the floor with an arm or book under their heads. If you prepare your students ahead of time, you can have them bring a small pillow into class. Students close their eyes and rest their attention on the soles of their feet. Notice and release any tension in that part of the body. Use the same "notice and release" techniques as students slowly move their attention through their calves, knees, thighs, pelvis, stomach, chest, shoulders, arms, neck, and head. After successfully completing this exercise, have your students take their seats. Students should repeat the exercise at their seats so that they feel comfortable performing it when they encounter stress in a classroom situation.

Stress Relief Have your students perform the breathing exercises in the checklist found on page 186 in Chapter 16, "Sixty Seconds to Relaxation."

Twenty Things I Like One way to relieve tension is to stop what one is doing and substitute a pleasant image for one's stressful thoughts and emotions. The purpose of this activity is to create a supply of pleasant thoughts and images to recall during a time of stress. Have each student conduct an eight-minute brainstorm to generate at least twenty things that he or she likes to do. When the list is completed, study it and pick out two or three activities that seem especially pleasant. Elaborate on them, and write down all of the memories that you have about them. Use these images to regain calm in stressful situations, such as exams.

Exam Questions Have each student bring in notes from the last several sessions of one of their classes. Or use the notes that your students have taken from the last several lectures that you have given. From these notes, have each student develop a list of test questions that he or she believes the instructor might ask on the next exam.

Group Exam Questions Have each student review his or her notes from several recent lectures. From these notes, students should create a list of questions that they believe will appear on the next exam. If your students attend a common core course or are part of a learning community, combine the lists of all students into a single comprehensive list. Distribute this final list to your students so they can use it to study for their next exam. Consider conducting a study session in one of your classes using this large list.

Getting Unstuck At some point, many students often encounter a test question about which they draw a blank and cannot seem to answer. Divide the class into small groups, and have each group develop as many ways to get unstuck as they can. In other words, each group should develop ways to move forward through the test by figuring out how to come up with something to write down when no immediate thoughts or answers present themselves. Each group should present its ideas to the class.

Timing a Test Develop small practice tests for the students in your class. The tests can be general-knowledge tests or tests of silly questions. Or you can use parts of old exams from your class. The goal of this activity is to help your students to feel more comfortable taking exams that must be completed within a certain time limit. Each test must be completed within a specified amount of time. The time allowed for each test should be brief. You are attempting to train your students to work under pressure in an environment that is not threatening to them and will not lower their grades.

Developing and Presenting Ideas

Chapter 20: Research: Defining What You Want to Discover

Writing well is an important skill in determining academic success and overall intelligence. Writing that is of high quality is the result of a process that involves many steps. And writing in college often includes some kind of research, research to find the answer to a question or solution to a problem, research to find information to support a theory or idea, or simply research to find a topic about which to write. No matter what a student does or what course of study she pursues, she will not be able to avoid some kind of research to support her writing at some point.

The first step in successful and effective writing is finding a subject about which to write. One must choose an appropriate and interesting topic, determine the question to be answered, or define the problem to be solved. Research can be an effective tool for all of these purposes. Chapter 20 describes the research and develops the methods that might be used to accomplish this initial, but most important, part of the writing process. In addition to using research to help choose a topic, this section then goes on to discuss how to refine one's topic selection, focus one's writing, and construct a thesis statement. It is important to take the time and put in the effort to carefully complete these preliminary steps, since successful accomplishing them will determine the quality of the writing that will follow.

This chapter will:

- explain the importance of conducting thorough research.
- teach students how to use brainstorming techniques to help choose appropriate topics.
- teach students how to refine the selection of their topics.
- discuss the importance of an effective thesis statement and teach students how to write one.
- teach students how to identify and clarify the purpose of their writing.
- discuss the importance of analyzing one's audience.

Suggestions for Teaching

Writing is a process that involves many steps. As desirable as it would be to simply sit down at a computer and create effective, exceptional writing, most people seldom can. Further, writing and research are bound together in most college courses. Chapters 20 through 24 of the *Master Student*

Guide focus on the complete writing process, with the first two chapters specifically addressing research and its relationship to and use in the writing process.

Consider beginning your introduction of Chapter 20 with an overview of the entire writing process so that students can understand the importance of each step and also see how each part of the process will develop and help to support those that come later. The goal of many students will be to finish a writing assignment as quickly as possible, thus tempting them to skip steps that they do not believe are necessary. This seldom results in a student's best writing. You can take this opportunity to develop your students' understanding of how a well-organized approach leads to an end product of higher quality.

Chapter 20 first introduces research into the writing process. However, formal research is not the focus of the chapter. (This is covered in detail in Chapter 21.) The focus of this chapter is the definition of a problem or the selection of a topic about which to write. Research is introduced in its capacity to support this initial part of the writing process.

Students may be quick to select a topic about which to write, making little use of the research techniques presented here. However, you should remind them that selection of the right topic is one of the most important steps in the process, since the topic that is chosen will drive all of the research and writing that will follow. As the *Guide* points out, time and care should be taken when choosing a topic for a college assignment.
Therefore, it can be an important advantage to perform some preliminary research to help in the selection of an appropriate topic. Chapter 20 provides many appropriate techniques and useful suggestions for this purpose.

This chapter continues by introducing the concept of the thesis statement. Remember that your students come from many diverse backgrounds, and the levels of their writing skills vary. Although they have all chosen or been assigned topics for writing in the past, some may not have been taught how to construct a thesis statement and may not realize the focus, clarity, and power that it can give to one's writing. Due to its influence and importance on the rest of a student's writing, consider paying special attention to this topic. Chapter 20 also develops a series of steps that focus on the development of a thesis statement and help a student to clarify the purpose and direction for which he or she is writing.

You can use many activities that will allow your students to practice and reinforce these skills. You can assign a very broad or vague topic on which to write and have your students select a specific topic within this category on which to write. For example, you could start with a broad topic such as a current political issue or obstacles to student success during the first year of college. Or if you are covering this chapter in support of your academic course, use your next writing assignment as an opportunity for students to choose their topics as a class activity. Or if you are teaching these sections as part of a learning community, you can have students bring in their next writing assignment from one of their core classes, and they can choose their topics as a class activity.

Consider approaching thesis statements in the same way. Provide some types of activities where your students write and/or critique thesis statements in class. You can assign topics for which students create a thesis statement. Or you can extend the previous assignments by having students go on to create thesis statements for the topics that they have chosen in prior activities.

I would suggest, however, that no matter which activities you assign, you consider having your students carry them out in class. This will allow you to observe and help them with the techniques that they use to research, brainstorm, choose and refine topics, and write thesis statements. From your perspective here, the techniques that are used are almost as important as the finished product. Remember that you will not be helping your students with every writing project that they are assigned. It is important that they develop their own sets of skills that will allow them to create work of high quality on their own. By completing all or most of these activities in class, you will be able to assist and guide them in the proper development of such skills.

Additional Activities and Exercises

Brainstorm a Topic Assign a broad topic to your class, such as the U.S. economy, success in the college student's first year, cloning, obstacles encountered by the adult nontraditional student, the European Union, and so on. Have each student perform an eight-minute brainstorming session to come up with as many essay topics as possible from the general topic that you assigned. Or you can divide the class into small groups and have each group brainstorm topics for ten minutes. The student or group that generates the most ideas is awarded a prize.

Search Engine Practice Assign ten to twelve broad topics (for example, conservation, pollution, religion, the European Union, IBM, France, the Olympics, chemistry, NASA, etc.). Have each student use at least three search engines to find five to ten sites, references, or sources from the Internet for each assigned topic.

Journalizing Topics Assign a single broad topic (such as NASA, cloning, the European Union, etc.) to your students. Have them complete one journal entry each day for one week. Each day, the student will narrow down the broad assigned topic to an idea for which it will be possible to write an essay. The journal entry will consist of the (first draft) introductory paragraph for this essay, including a thesis statement. By the end of the week, each student will have developed five essay ideas from the general topic that was assigned.

Critiquing Thesis Statements This exercise is a continuation of "Journalizing Topics." Divide the class into small groups. Each student should bring to class the five thesis statements that he or she wrote for the journalizing activity. Each group member should read his or her statements and have the other group members critique them for clarity and conciseness.

Assign a Paper Assign a broad writing topic to your class, such as one of those suggested in one of the other exercises. Have each student complete all of the steps in the beginning stages of the writing process as described in Chapter 20 of the *Master Student Guide.* Each student should begin by brainstorming essay ideas, narrowing down the list of appropriate topics, researching and refining the topic, choosing a topic, establishing a purpose for the paper, and writing an effective thesis statement. Evaluate each student's work at each step of the process.

Plagiarism and Its Consequences Conduct a discussion about plagiarism and its consequences. Include the possible failure of a course, expulsion from college, and the recent authors and newspaper writers who have been accused of plagiarism.

Analyze the Audience Decide on several types of audiences for whom your students will be "writing" a paper. (You could choose parents, businesspeople, doctors, and elementary school students, for example). Divide the class into small groups. Each group should develop a profile or list of characteristics of the groups to whom it will be writing. Have each group present one of its profiles to the class.

Chapter 21: Research: Using Sources and Information

Many writing projects will be assigned throughout the course of a student's college life. Some type of research will be required to support and supplement many of these projects. The abilities to define clearly the questions that need to be answered for a project (Chapter 20), to determine the appropriate sources to be used to find or develop these answers, and to access efficiently these sources in order to conduct the required research, all enable students to carry out the writing process easily and successfully. Chapter 21 provides a variety of methods and resources with which students can learn how to accomplish these goals.

This chapter will:

- help to identify the many sources of research available to students.
- define primary and secondary resources and explain the differences between the two.
- teach students how to evaluate sources (including those found on the Internet) critically in order to determine their quality.
- provide a list of important reference sources (see the sidebar "Reference Works – Print and Online" on page 246 and the sidebar "Dig into the Invisible Web" on page 248).
- introduce the topics of paraphrasing, quotation, and plagiarism.

Suggestions for Teaching

The material presented in Chapter 21 is fairly straightforward. Your goal will be to teach your students how to conduct research. Although all of your students will have written papers before, remember that some students may not have conducted research before, may not have done very much research, or may not have conducted research very well. Although students may tell you that they know how to write and/or that they know how to conduct research, many may not, in fact, understand the research process or possess good research skills.

I would suggest beginning your lessons on this chapter by explaining the importance of research to the writing process. You can explain to your students how research enhances and strengthens writing by providing clarity, detail, direction, and support for one's thesis, argument, or opinion. Next, you can explain that conducting research is a systematic process and describe the process. The process begins by correctly identifying or defining the questions to be answered (see Chapter 20). In other words, what is the purpose for which the student is carrying out this research? Obviously, this helps to direct the student to the type of research that will be needed. Is the needed information new? Or has it been researched and published before? Where can the student find this information? Although this process may seem clear to you, research for many students consists of going to the library and looking up the chosen topic with no more direction or thought. They simply use whatever they happen to find for their assignments. Obviously, your review of a systematic approach will be of benefit.

Within the research process, the majority of a student's time can be taken up by looking for the right sources of information. In other words, "I know what I want. Where do I find it?" Hours can easily be wasted trying to find the answers and information that one needs with little direction or purpose. One of the most important things that you can teach your students is where to go to look for different kinds of research information. Take advantage of the excellent listings and descriptions of resource information that this chapter provides. Use them to help teach your students how to decide which resources might be most appropriate and productive for different purposes. These tools will prove invaluable over the course of your students' lives, in college, in the workplace, and in their personal lives.

Also, remember to explain to your students that not all research is of the same quality and that it is important to evaluate the research that they find and use. Chapter 21 also provides detail and insight into the evaluation process. Finally, it is a good idea to discuss plagiarism and its consequences.

Consider assigning activities and exercises to increase your students' understanding of the techniques that you have taught them. The initial approach to reinforce their mastery of research methods is fairly simple: have them conduct some research. Assign a topic to be researched (see the "Search Engine Practice" activity that follows for a list of possible topics), give a writing assignment that will require some type of research in order to complete it, or have your students use a real writing assignment that they have been given in one of their other academic classes. No matter which exercise you choose, evaluate the process that they use, the techniques that they choose, and the quality of the research that results from their efforts.

Additional Activities and Exercises

Library Tour Arrange for your students to take a comprehensive tour of the library that includes demonstrations of reference and research materials and equipment.

Search Engine Practice Assign ten to twelve broad topics (for example, conservation, pollution, religion, the European Union, IBM, France, the Olympics, chemistry, NASA, etc.). Have each student use at least three search engines to find five to ten sites, references, or sources from the Internet for each assigned topic.

Plagiarism and Its Consequences Conduct a discussion about plagiarism and its consequences. Include the possible failure of a course, expulsion from college, and the recent authors and newspaper writers who have been accused of plagiarism.

Interview Have each student conduct primary research by interviewing someone. Each student should interview a local businessperson or someone who is employed by a local company about his or her career. Students should ask questions such as the educational and other special skill requirements of the job, length of employment, career path, enjoyment of the job, level of education completed, and the like. Each student should submit a short essay based on the information obtained from the interview.

Chapter 22: Preparing to Write

The *Master Student Guide to Academic Success* correctly points out that writing is not simply a matter of "*knowing* what you think and then transcribing it to paper." Writing would be so easy for everyone if this was the case. Rather, writing is actually a process of *discovering* what one wants to say. This process of discovery will include experimenting, exploring, following different paths, and accepting some leads while rejecting others.

Good writing does not just happen when one sits down in front of a computer. There is much planning and preparation that should take place before and during the writing process. Chapter 20 developed the first preliminary steps (topic selection, development of the thesis statement, etc.) that should take place prior to the actual writing. Chapter 22 now focuses more fully on the planning process and completes the organization and preparation that one needs in order to fully attack one's writing and produce high-quality results.

This chapter will:

- introduce and describe the three steps of the writing process.
- teach students how to plan a writing project.
- explain the importance of a writing schedule, and teach students how to set one up (see the checklist on page 256).
- Explain the importance of setting up an outline, and teach students how to create one.

- Explain the importance of the introduction (see the sidebar "Creating an Inviting Introduction" on p. 258).
- Introduce the method of collaborative writing and review.

Suggestions for Teaching

Many students are their own worst enemies when it comes to writing. They want to spend as little time writing as possible. Their ideal writing method consists of sitting down, writing a single complete draft, and handing in a paper that hopefully receives an "A". As previously pointed out, this is rarely the method that produces writing of high quality. Building on this realization, you could introduce your lesson by describing the many disadvantages of using a method such as this and continue on to explain the many benefits of a process-centered approach to writing. This introduction can then flow smoothly into a description of each of the three stages of the writing process (as described in the *Master Student Guide*): prewriting, writing, and revising.

Remember to point out to your students that although writing is usually presented as a process that consists of a series of steps (as is done in this book), it is actually a very personal process. That is, different people may go through the steps in a different order, start and stop, and return to previously worked-on steps. This is all acceptable. Writing is personal and fluid. What is most important is that one goes through *all* the steps when writing. It is fine, even suggested, to rearrange the steps to suit one's own personal preferences. Just do them all.

Chapter 22 provides many excellent ideas that will help your students to plan and structure a personal writing process that can lead to efficiency in its execution and quality in its final product. You can and should take advantage of many or all of them, but I suggest that you always include and emphasize outlining in your lessons.

I make this suggestion because I have discovered that the last thing that many students will ever choose to do when writing is to use an outline. You might counter that your students are now in college and that they must have learned how to create and use outlines somewhere in their past academic experience. One would think so. However, somehow they seem to do everything that they possibly can to avoid this exercise in writing preparation. They seem to sleep, write letters, go to the bathroom, and get sick and stay home when it is being taught. They always tell their teachers that they have used them in their papers, but seldom do. It seems that they only produce them when absolutely necessary, that is, when they are required to hand one in along with an actual writing assignment.

So, in many cases, these are the attitudes and skills possessed (or perhaps not possessed) by the students that you now find in your classes. It will be your responsibility to convince your students to include outlining as one of the steps in their writing processes. You can explain the added direction and organization that outlining builds into writing. It helps to act as a road map that can guide one more directly to a destination, especially if one becomes bored or confused while writing. To this end, it also helps provide a quick but full picture of one's writing project, especially those assignments of considerable length (which most college students will surely encounter eventually). Finally, skill in outlining ultimately saves time. By increasing organization, providing direction, and producing a whole picture made up of readily observable pieces, a short amount of time spent creating an outline before writing can save a great deal of time that might have been spent aimlessly wandering through writing.

Also, you might find it useful to discuss the importance of the introduction. You can remind your students that they can even write this crucial piece at the end of the process. Many students get stuck writing in sequence. This is not a requirement in writing. Sometimes it is easier to write the beginning at the end, especially if one does not know exactly where one is going to wind up when one starts. Remember that writing is a process of discovery. Sometimes it is OK to write the end before one writes the beginning.

You can consider teaching a lesson on collaborative writing and review. Many students will not have considered writing with someone else. You can help introduce them to the benefits of such a technique. In addition, many college projects are of significant length and are assigned to a group. You can help prepare your students for the possibility of such a situation, the potential obstacles that they might encounter, and the interpersonal relationships and variety of skill levels that they will need to manage in such a project.

Finally, you can point out that students should have at least one person review and edit their writing. It is almost impossible to be objective about one's own work. It is important to build this added quality into the process. The achievement of high-quality writing is too important to one's academic success to neglect this critical step.

The activities that can be assigned to develop and reinforce the skills in this chapter are almost endless (see the section that follows for some suggestions). They can include outlining, planning, organizing, scheduling, editing, and collaborating. They can be independent assignments, part of another formal writing project that you have assigned but are assessing separately, or an assignment that is based on a writing project that students have been assigned in one of their other academic classes or in another class that is part of their learning community.

Additional Activities and Exercises

Writing Schedule Have each student identify an upcoming writing assignment in one of his or her courses. Or you could assign a writing project in your class (such as an autobiography, an interview with someone a student admires, a career analysis and plan, a summary of some current event, etc.). Each student should create a writing schedule for the identified writing assignment. The writing process should take place over several days or weeks. The schedule will map out each of the steps that must be completed in the process and when they are to be done in order to submit a quality writing assignment on time. Have your students submit their writing assignment to you for review and comment.

Outlining Have each student identify an upcoming writing assignment in one of their courses. Or you could assign a writing project in your class (such as an autobiography, an interview with someone a student admires, a career analysis and plan, a summary of some current event, etc.). Each student should construct an outline for the identified writing assignment. Have your students submit their writing assignment to you for review and comment.

Edit I Divide your class into pairs of students. Have each student bring in the most recent writing assignment that he or she has completed for your course or one of his or her other courses. Do not allow them to select what they consider to be their best writing of the semester. They *must* bring whichever essay or project is their most *recent* writing assignment. If a student has a nearly completed paper or essay that he or she is about to submit, he or she can use that assignment. Have the partners in each group switch papers and edit the others' work.

Edit II This is a variation of the Edit I exercise. Have each student bring in the most recent short writing assignment that they have completed for your course or one of their other courses. Do not allow them to select what they consider to be their best writing of the semester. They *must* bring whichever essay or project is their most *recent* writing assignment. If a student has a nearly completed paper or essay that he or she is about to submit, he or she can use that assignment. Collect the assignments. Make five copies of each paper. Divide the class into groups of four students. Return the papers and the copies to the original authors. Have each of the groups edit and critique the papers of each of the four group members.

Building Introductions Have each student identify an upcoming writing assignment in one of his or her courses. Or you could assign a writing project in your class (such as an autobiography, an interview with someone a student admires, a career analysis and plan, a summary of some current event, etc.). For this assignment, students do not have to write an entire paper. Each student must only write an introduction. The introduction must be focused, explain the purpose of the paper, attract the attention of the reader, and encourage the reader to continue into the body of the essay. Have students submit their finished introductions to you or to a partner for review.

Collaborative Writing The focus of this writing activity is to help students feel more comfortable in their writing by allowing them to create an essay as a member of a group instead of relying only on their own ideas and writing skills. Divide the class into groups. Have the group members identify an upcoming writing assignment in one of their courses. Or you could assign a writing project in your class (such as an autobiography, an interview with someone a student admires, a career analysis and plan, a summary of some current event, etc.). For this exercise, the assignment should only be one or two pages long. Have the group write the paper together.

As a variation on this assignment, the group could use a free-writing type project. For example, you could give them the beginning phrase of a story, such as "Once upon a time …" or "The man left his house early in the morning...". The group would then be required to complete an entire story of at least one to two pages in length. The story must make sense and contain a clear beginning, middle, and ending. Have each group read its story to the class. Follow the reading with a discussion of the advantages and disadvantages that each group encountered in this type of writing.

Chapter 23: Writing a Draft

Every significant writing project at the college level requires at least two drafts. This fact is not what many students like to hear. The completion of multiple drafts of a project obviously takes more time than producing a single draft. And the demands on the time of college students are great. They may be tempted or need to work overtime to complete an important project at their jobs, study for an exam in another class, take a son or daughter to the park, go to the gym, help a daughter with homework, sleep, or go to a fraternity party.

Writing well, however, is a skill that lasts a lifetime, is used for many purposes, and is needed in many different careers. Most importantly, the ability to communicate effectively brings great academic, career, and personal success.

Unfortunately, writing of any significant quality, no matter how gifted and skilled the creator, will never be produced in a single draft. However, if one takes the time to execute carefully and fully the planning and prewriting stages, much of the hard work of writing has been completed. Students can then relax into the writing of their first drafts.

This chapter will:

- introduce techniques to reduce students' resistance to writing.
- suggest ways to overcome writer's block.
- explain the importance of finishing a first draft quickly.
- explain the importance of distance (from a draft).

Suggestions for Teaching

You will probably want to consider two main objectives as you focus on the topics in this chapter: convincing your students of the many benefits that result from the use of multiple drafts and reducing their resistance to writing. As you have seen, Chapters 20 through 22 of the *Master Student Guide*, as well as the corresponding sections of the Instructor's Resource Manual, provide many arguments for the former. In order to address the latter, you might begin by asking why students are resistant to writing. The most common answers are probably a lack of time or because they believe that they are not good at it. *The Guide* provides many ways for students to become better organized, balance their many competing responsibilities more effectively, and manage their time more efficiently.

One of your greatest remaining challenges, then, is to build confidence in your students' abilities to write well. Whether you believe that writing is an art or a skill, the way in which one develops it and gets better at it is through practice. Therefore, you should have your students write. This chapter (23) provides a great variety of techniques with which to encourage and facilitate your students' writing of a first draft.

Further, here are some key points that are reviewed briefly to help lessen your students' resistance to the writing process. Encourage them to write regularly, about anything. They should force themselves to fill up a blank page with whatever comes to mind. Several times each week they should write about anything until at least one page is completely filled. Such routine and discipline provides practice and helps remove barriers to poor writing. In other words, not all writing has to be perfect. This is a first draft, not a final version. The writing does not always have to be good the first time around.

Point out to your students that they can get physical. That is, they can get up and walk around. They do not have to be chained to a desk. If they are using a laptop, they have many locations available in which to write. Students can even get up, go outside, and take a walk if they are having trouble coming up with words and ideas. In short, students should not be afraid to relax and take advantage of situations and environments that might help to enhance their thinking and creativity.

Similarly, remind your students to experience new things and put themselves in unfamiliar situations. Go to a foreign film. Try a new sport. See a play. Go to an art museum. Don't be afraid to try new things; they can inspire creativity. The greater the variety of experiences, the more one has to draw upon when writing.

Remind your students to write quickly. This will be a first draft, not a final one. They will be able to, in fact they must, revise the draft later. Quality and perfection are not the goals here. Here, the goal is to commit a complete first draft to paper. Since they will *definitely* revise later, why spend too much time trying to perfect this very first draft?

Finally, advise your students to put some distance between themselves and the draft. They must let it sit for at least several hours (preferably several days) before they revise and edit. It is important to put a draft aside and then revisit it later in order to look at it with fresh eyes. They need to remember to schedule enough time into the writing process so that they can let the draft rest as described.

Now, have your students write!

Additional Activities and Exercises

Free Writing Have each student take out several blank pieces of paper. Have them start to write and continue writing without stopping for eight minutes. They can write about anything. Walk around the room and make sure that no one stops writing. Have your students discuss their results and how they felt about the exercise. As a variation, you could have them begin with a partial sentence such as: "In order to save the world, I will…"; "I am the best person because…"; "Tomorrow, I will…".

Short Essays In class, have each student write a one-page essay on a topic that you assign, submitting the essay at the end of class or the end of the designated time period. Suggested topics: Should we go back to the moon?; a news story from the front page of this morning's newspaper; why the commercials during the Super Bowl are better than the game; my favorite animal is…; the President of the United States should/should not be reelected; I would like to live in…

Writing Drills Conduct weekly writing drills in your class for three to six weeks. Assign a topic on which your students will write for fifteen to twenty minutes once each week. (See the preceding "Short Essays" exercise for a list of possible topics.)

Journal Writing Have each student keep a writing journal for a month or for the entire semester. Require one or two entries to be completed each week. Each entry should be at least one page in length and can focus on a topic assigned by the instructor or chosen by the student, at the instructor's discretion. The journal should be submitted to or checked by the instructor periodically.

Collaborative Writing The focus of this writing activity is to help students feel more comfortable in their writing by allowing them to create an essay as a member of a group instead of relying only on their own ideas and writing skills. Divide the class into groups. Have the group members identify an upcoming writing assignment in one of their courses. Or you could assign a writing project in your class (such as an autobiography, an interview with someone a student admires, a career analysis and plan, a summary of some current event, etc.). For this exercise, the assignment should only be one or two pages long. Have the group write the paper together. As a variation on this assignment, the group could use a free-writing type project. For example, you could give them the beginning phrase of a story, such as "Once upon a time…" or "The man left his house early in the morning ...". The group would then be required to complete an entire story of at least one to two pages in length. The story must make sense and contain a clear beginning, middle, and end. Have each group read its story to the class. Follow the reading with a discussion of the advantages and disadvantages that each group encountered in this type of writing.

Something New Require each student to do something new this week. For example, go home using a different route; watch a television show that had not been seen before; shop in a new store; or go to a place, such as a lake, library, or museum, that had not been visited before. Then have each student write a short essay describing why they chose what they did, and describing the new things they saw or learned.

Chapter 24: Revising Your Draft

The final, but no less important, step in the writing process is revision. Although Chapter 23 advocates writing quickly to complete a first draft, when one edits and revises it is time to slow down and examine one's work carefully. It is at this stage that one has the final, and perhaps greatest, opportunity to build cohesiveness and quality into one's work.

This chapter will:

- explain the importance of revision to the writing process.
- explain the importance of obtaining feedback about one's writing from others.
- identify and describe important editing techniques.

Suggestions for Teaching

If you have convinced your students of the necessity of completing more than one draft when writing, then you have already convinced them of the importance of revision. After all, the purpose of the second, third, or fourth draft of a paper is its improvement. That improvement, or enhanced quality, is achieved through the writing/editing process.

As stated previously, a first draft should be written quickly in order to capture one's major thoughts and create a skeleton or frame of what the essay, paper, or project will be. Revision, however, is a much slower process. Now, quality will be built into the writing. Much more care and attention will be focused on getting the writing exactly right. It is probably even a good idea to think of reviewing each subsequent draft to an even greater level of detail, and, therefore, each draft will be revised at an even slower pace than the previous one.

Chapter 24 addresses many of the important areas to consider when revising one's writing and provides ideas about how best to approach each of them in order to enhance the quality of one's writing. Remind students to focus on clarity, grammar, spelling, punctuation, and the overall flow of the material. Upon reading the entire paper, is it too wordy or verbose? Does there appear to be something missing from certain sections, or is there a gap where there should be something linking related ideas together? Does the introduction draw the reader in and make her want to continue reading? Does the conclusion make a definitive statement or clearly summarize the paper or does it just fade off?

Although you may not be teaching an English course or using this chapter as part of an English lesson, you should keep in mind that many students struggle with grammar, punctuation, or sentence construction. With this in mind, you will find six of the most common sentence errors on page 275. You might consider reviewing these with your students since they are committed frequently and are relatively easy to correct through awareness and practice.

It is also important to convince your students of the value of getting feedback from others about their writing. Students *should* share their work with others. However, this will be a challenge for some. After all, writing is somewhat personal. It can be thought of as putting part of yourself onto paper or into a computer file. It is not always easy for students to share this with others, especially when it is an incomplete draft that almost certainly contains errors. You should try to help your students get over this because the benefits gained far outweigh any insecurities held by the writer. Editors are almost always aware of the fact that they are not looking at a completed, perfect document, and few are judgmental or condescending. They will, however, often find mistakes and errors that the writer has missed. An editor's fresh perspective allows him to see things to which familiarity has blinded the writer. What is clear to the author may not be clear to the reader. Editing by another allows the student to find and correct such inconsistencies and unclear thoughts before submitting a final version to his professor.

Finally, you can remind your students that they should make sure that their papers meet the requirements for submission. For example, if a professor has stated that a paper should be double spaced with page numbers in the top right-hand corner and a single-stapled cover page, a student should not hand in a paper that is single spaced, numbered at the bottom, and stuffed inside a store-bought report cover. The assignment should be submitted in the way the instructor wants, not the way the student likes. The instructor has reasons for the way in which she wants a paper formatted, and it is the instructor who is giving out the grade. It is important to conform to these standards so one doesn't lose points from one's grade after working so hard to turn in a high-quality paper.

As always, you will want your students to practice revision. There are many ways to accomplish this, but it will be of great benefit if your students can bring to class a writing assignment on which they are currently working for another course. This will allow your students to practice these skills in a real way in which they can quickly see the benefit in the grade earned on the next writing assignment that they submit.

Additional Activities and Exercises

Writing Schedule Have each student identify an upcoming writing assignment in one of his or her courses. Or you could assign a writing project in your class (such as an autobiography, an interview with someone a student admires, a career analysis and plan, a summary of some current event, etc.). After writing the first draft for either of these assignments, have the students bring this draft to class. Have each student carefully proofread and revise his or her first draft. You may even want to have students submit the final draft of the essay as well as the first draft for comparison.

Short Essays Have each student write a one-page essay on a topic that you assign. This essay should be completed in class and submitted at the end of the class period or the end of the designated time period. Suggested topics: Should we go back to the moon?; a news story from the front page of this morning's newspaper; why the commercials during the Super Bowl are better than the game; my favorite animal is…; the President of the United States should/should not be reelected; I would like to live in…
Return the essays, and have each student carefully edit and revise his or her work. Students should submit the final draft of the essay, as well as the first draft for comparison.

Edit I Divide your class into pairs of students. Have each student bring in the most recent writing assignment that he or she has completed for your course or another course. Do not allow them to select what they consider to be their best writing of the semester. They *must* bring whichever essay or project is their most *recent* writing assignment. If a student has a nearly completed paper or essay that he or she is about to submit, he or she can use that assignment. Have the partners in each group switch papers and edit the other's work.

Edit II This is a variation of the Edit I exercise. Have each student bring in the most recent short writing assignment that he or she has completed for your course or another course. Do not allow them to select what they consider to be their best writing of the semester. They *must* bring whichever essay or project is their most *recent* writing assignment. If a student has a nearly completed paper or essay that he or she is about to submit, he or she can use that assignment. Collect the assignments. Make five copies of each paper. Divide the class into groups of four students. Return the papers and the copies to the original authors. Have each of the groups edit and critique the papers of each of the four group members.

Read for Six Common Sentence Errors Have each student bring in the draft of an upcoming writing assignment that is due in one of their courses. Or he or she can bring in one of his or her recently submitted writing assignments. Review the assignment, and identify any of the six common sentence errors described on page 275 of Chapter 24 in the *Master Student Guide*. Divide the class into pairs of students. Have each student switch papers with his or her partner, and have the partner look for and identify any of the six common sentence errors that might have been missed during the first revision.

Chapter 25: Making Effective Presentations

Public speaking is considered by many to be one of the most difficult and stressful situations that they could encounter. Many popular surveys conducted in recent years rush to point out that people find speaking in front of others more intimidating and stressful than most other major life events, including such things as divorce and even death!

However, success in college and the workplace is dependent, in large part, on effective communication. Speaking in public as a participant in a group, in front of a classroom, in meetings, as the leader of a group, or in more formal and larger situations is part of the communications process. The best communicators, across these different formats, are often those who are most successful at school, work, and life. Therefore, it is important to overcome this anxiety and fear of speaking in public--as much as is possible anyway. As many teachers, actors, and businesspeople know, it is usually impossible to completely eliminate nervousness in front of a group. However, there are many things that can be done to manage it.

There are really only two areas on which to focus to reduce or overcome the fear and anxiety associated with public speaking: practice and preparation. Both can build confidence in one's potential success, which can help to make one less nervous. Reduced nervousness and associated stress and anxiety helps one to make a better speech or presentation. This, in turn, builds more confidence in one's speaking ability, which reduces nervousness and stress. All of which, hopefully, leads to the development of a better public speaker.

This chapter will:

- help students to become better public speakers through organization, preparation, and practice.
- introduce the key elements of planning a presentation.
- teach students how to plan a presentation.
- discuss the importance of the introduction to a speech or presentation.
- discuss the importance and creation of support materials to speeches and presentations.
- discuss the importance of rehearsal or practice and introduce key elements of the practice process.
- introduce effective presentation techniques.

Suggestions for Teaching

Almost everyone, not just students, fears speaking in front of others to some degree. As previously stated, much success in school, career, and life is due to the ability to communicate effectively. One of the essential skills of communication is public speaking. Since one of your goals is to help students to become successful, it is important for you to help them to overcome some of this fear of speaking in public and to help them to improve this valuable skill.

In order for your students to achieve this goal, they must prepare and practice. The next section suggests many activities that provide practice opportunities for your students. However, it will be up to you to find the time within your schedule to use these exercises. A single speech will not be sufficient to overcome their anxiety or develop their skill. Although there is much other material to cover in your course, try to find ways to have your students present information and lessons to the class whenever possible. Look for chances throughout the semester where you can combine a presentation with another lesson or project. After all, your students must practice, practice, practice!!

Next, remember that preparation builds confidence. A student is much more likely to make a successful presentation if he knows what he wants to say, how he wants to say it, to whom he is saying it, and actually rehearses saying it. Chapter 25 develops a process that will take your students through each of these important steps. You can take advantage of the clear steps and suggestions contained here and structure a lesson that easily carries students from topic selection through to practice and presentation.

Once you have completed such a lesson, consider having your students make a speech and follow them through each step of the preparation process. You can assign a topic (such as ways to get promoted at your job, the benefits of sending people to the moon, the reality of global warming, how to study for an "A"), or allow your students to choose their own. Have your students complete most of the preparation for this speech in the classroom so you can ensure that they are completing all steps and not omitting any. Finally, after each student presents his or her speech, remember to provide feedback. Although practice leads to improvement, it is especially difficult for students to evaluate their own performances since they cannot see themselves as they present. Therefore, you might consider videotaping a set of speeches or presentations, if possible. Watching themselves, no matter how resistant they are (and they will be resistant) to this idea, will provide the most effective feedback and lead to lasting improvement.

Additional Activities and Exercises

Introductions Have each student in your class introduce him or herself to the rest of the class. Students should tell the class something about themselves, such as where they are from, where they work, their course of study, special interests, and the like. Students should address the class from the front of the classroom.

Extemporaneous Speeches Have each student give a two-minute extemporaneous or impromptu speech. Suggested topics: my favorite movie, my best vacation, my favorite novel, what I did last weekend, my hobby, the last movie that I saw, what animal I would choose to be, how to achieve academic success.

Speeches Have each student prepare and deliver a formal three- to five-minute speech to the class. Provide feedback to each student at the conclusion of his or her speech. Consider videotaping the speeches if possible. Suggested topics: should we send people to Mars?; how to tie a tie; why I should be elected student government representative; should we allow oil drilling in the Arctic National Wildlife Refuge?; the best sport in the world is….

Create an Introduction Divide the class into groups. Have each group select from a list of topics, such as those listed in the preceding "Speeches" exercise, or assign a topic to each group. Group members should collectively write an effective introduction for the speech topic that was assigned. One group member should present the introduction to the class.

Create Your Notes Assign a topic for a speech or presentation to each student. (See suggested topics in the earlier "Speeches" exercise.) Have each student create speaking notes for the speech that he or she will deliver (see the checklist on page 280). Review each student's set of notes to ensure that they are appropriate and acceptable.

Group Presentations Divide the class into groups. Assign a presentation that each group will be required to deliver in one or two weeks. Each group member must participate in the presentation. Suggested topics: the best thing about College ABC is…; why we should/should not send people to the moon; why outsourcing jobs to India is/is not a bad thing for the U.S. economy; should there be a family hour of programming on network television?

Current Events Research Bring your class to the library. Have each student find a short article from a recent newspaper or magazine. Students should copy their chosen articles. Have each student prepare a three-minute speech based on the article and present it during the next class meeting. Remember to give feedback to each student after his or her speech.

Regular Current Events Require each student to summarize and present articles about current events periodically throughout the semester. Each student should deliver three to five short presentations.

Chapter 26: Using Computers to Promote Your Success

Computers are now a part of almost everyone's life in some way. They are certainly a part of every student's academic life. The use and mastery of these recently ubiquitous machines is probably just as important to students' academic success as the ability to think, speak, read, and write well.

On every college campus today, the presence of computers, small and large and for dozens of purposes, is just as much of a requirement as is a library. One would not consider attending a school without a library. Neither would one consider attending a college that was not connected to the world and internally via computers. Computers can be found from computer labs to classrooms to the library. Dormitories increasingly are wired to handle the additional power demands placed on their electrical systems by students who have computers in their rooms. Some colleges even require students to purchase their own computers as part of enrollment and attendance in their programs.

The power that computing gives to students is undeniable. Its access to information, its ability to enhance communication, its word processing and calculating power, and its support of and flexibility for study and test-taking methods, among many other uses, make the computer a vital part of any student's academic success. This chapter (26) introduces the many ways that computers can contribute to academic success, and Chapter 27 will specifically address Internet resources available to students and ways they can connect to the online community.

This chapter will:

- introduce students to and remind them of the many uses of computers in higher education.
- help students to identify and evaluate their own college computing requirements, including whether or not they should or need to purchase their own computers.
- teach students how to evaluate the computer resources available on campus.
- suggest ways to integrate computers and information technology into daily study tasks.
- explain the importance of protecting one's computer files and introduce the basic methods of doing so.

Suggestions for Teaching

Unlike some of the other areas addressed in the *Master Student Guide*, this is one in which many of your students will possess much knowledge and experience. In fact, a traditional first-year student, through his use of the Internet, instant messaging, chat rooms, cell phones, Internet research, personal digital assistants, and MP3 players, may be just as knowledgeable (or perhaps even more so) in his use of computers as you are.

The nontraditional student may be less comfortable in her level of computer knowledge, although this is less often the case nowadays than it was ten years ago since the presence of computers in many workplaces has greatly increased the level of basic computer literacy for a great number of people.

In any case, Chapter 26 provides an opportunity for you to review computer basics for your students and quickly inventory their level of computer comfort and knowledge. In turn, this assessment will allow you to properly address your students' levels of computer knowledge and to plan any lessons needed to accommodate particular gaps in your students' computer skills.

You could begin this section with a very quick introduction to computers, their history, hardware, software, peripherals, and so on. This discussion then can continue on to the computer's place on the college campus and its many uses in this setting. As this chapter details, you could discuss criteria to decide whether a student should bring (or purchase) his or her own computer to campus. Further, if a student ultimately decides to do so, the chapter discusses what hardware and software requirements should be considered in the computer that he purchases or brings with him. Within the context of this discussion, you could also provide information about the computer resources that are already available on campus for student use, such as computer availability and access, online registration, Internet rules and access, distance education courses offered by the college, online access to student information and grades, and so on.

As stated, it is a good idea to quickly inventory your students' level of computer knowledge and skill. After all, this is a key determinant of student success. And although many students are now computer literate, one does not want to make the assumption that this same high level of literacy applies to everyone. If some of your students do require additional information and guidance in this area, it is important to uncover this need and provide the direction and support that will enhance their skills here (just as would be done in any other academic skill area).

This inventory could be a quick series of questions asked in class. Or if you fear that some students would be too intimidated to reveal a lack of knowledge in front of classmates, you could use a short written instrument. Consider addressing areas such as knowledge of basic hardware and software, Internet knowledge, and use of certain program applications, Internet and e-mail, and online resources.

You could go on to include a discussion of the ways that computer technology can enhance basic learning strategies, such as note- and test-taking. Note that if you have taught many of the previous chapters prior to this lesson, you may have already discussed methods by which computers can contribute to the enhancement of academic skills and would consequently omit such a lesson here.

Finally, you should consider a quick lesson on basic methods to protect one's computer files (see the checklist on page 292). Discuss the importance of frequently saving one's work, backing up or saving one's files in more than one place, and virus protection software. It is extremely frustrating to work for hours and then lose that work because one has not saved it, backed it up to a second file, or protected one's computer from a virus that crashes it or erases the file. Too many of us have been in these situations, and it is the last thing that a busy student needs to experience.

Internet resources and the online community are covered in Chapter 27. You may choose to cover this chapter separately, or you might combine it in a lesson with Chapter 26, since this chapter may have been covered relatively quickly.

Additional Activities and Exercises

Campus Computer Inventory Have your students compile a list of all computer resources available to students both on and off campus at the college. Include all sites and methods of computer access available to students both on and off campus. This activity can be completed individually or in small groups.

My Computer Background Using word processing software, have each student write a one-page paper describing his or her computer background and access to computer facilities. Include these headings: Computer education – computer courses or use of computers in courses that he or she has taken; Hardware – type of equipment that he or she will be using this semester; Software – application software that he or she knows how to use; Strengths – knowledge and skills about which he or she feels confident

Computer Benefits Conduct a class discussion that develops a list of all the ways that computers can help a student to enhance his or her academic success.

Chapter 27: Becoming a Member of the Online Community

As computers have become an increasingly common part of many areas of our lives, the Internet also has greatly influenced the ways in which people communicate and interact with others, especially in the academic world. Not only is the Internet a tool for research (Chapters 20 and 21), but it is also a way to link people together and enhance communication between them.

Chapter 27 describes and introduces students to the online community, as well as explaining some of its most common uses and the many potential benefits for students who participate in it. The power of information and communication is great, and the Internet and the online community can do much to enhance this power. All students should take advantage of this tool and its resources. This chapter tells students how to become members of this new community (if they have not done so already).

This chapter will:

- introduce students to the online community.
- explain the advantages of using e-mail.
- teach students how to write effectively for an online receiver.
- describe e-mail lists, newsgroups, and chat rooms and explain the potential benefits of each.
- explain the concept of distance learning.
- provide a checklist to help determine a student's readiness and potential ability to benefit from distance learning.

Suggestions for Teaching

Research, including the use of the Internet as a resource for this purpose, is covered in Chapters 20 and 21. This chapter (27) introduces students to the online community and its many faces and uses in addition to that of research tool.

Consider beginning your lesson with a discussion of the many obvious benefits gained by becoming a member of and participant in the online community. For example, the ability to connect with and establish relationships with other people throughout the world is obviously extremely valuable in the academic and business worlds. In addition, the Internet provides access to more information and enables that information and knowledge to be transferred and spread more easily and quickly than ever before.

Next, you should probably take an inventory of the number of students who are already active participants in the online community. In a class made up of traditional students, you will probably find that they have already incorporated e-mail, chat rooms, instant messaging, and search engines into their daily lives. Nontraditional students have probably done so but to a lesser extent and may feel less familiar with the range of options available online. Some students may be entirely unfamiliar with most of these resources. Question your students further in order to determine which of these tools they know how to use and do so on a regular basis. The purpose here is not to intimidate students by disclosing gaps in their experience, but to gain feedback so you know how quickly to cover this material and how to structure the lessons and activities in this section.

Regardless of your students' Internet experience, it is probably a good idea to review several key topics. Many students will use the Internet in their everyday lives and may have developed habits, shortcuts, and slang that are inappropriate in a more formal situation such as an academic classroom or business office. Consider including a lesson on e-mail etiquette or netiquette. (See the sidebar "A Brief Guide to Netiquette" on page 301.) Remind your students of the importance of brevity in e-mail correspondence and the differences between traditional writing and writing for e-mail.

If needed, describe different parts of the online community, such as newsgroups, chat rooms, and instant messaging. Consider providing a list of different search engines and conducting a quick lesson on their use. Depending on the backgrounds and experiences of your students, you might assign several lessons for them to practice such things as composing appropriate e-mail messages or using search engines properly. Also consider a brief discussion of the concept of distance learning, the distance-learning options available through your college, and the abilities and characteristics of students who will most successfully use and benefit from this resource.

Finally, although most of you have probably already done so, you should utilize the Internet and participate in the online community in order to enhance your classroom. Take advantage of the easy communication and accessibility between you and your students that e-mail provides. Post your course information, such as your syllabus or perhaps even class notes, on the Internet. Take advantage of online instructional resources, such as those provided by Houghton Mifflin and other textbook publishers. Search the Internet for groups and activities that will enhance your teaching and your courses. Remember that one of the best ways to teach is by example. The more "wired" that you are, the more comfortable your students will be.

Additional Activities and Exercises

Online Correspondence Provide your students with various situations for which they must compose appropriate e-mail messages using proper netiquette: for example, a request for a job interview, an apology for having missed a professor's class, and a request for information from a business.

E-Mail Me If you feel that many of your students do not have much experience using the Internet, then have each one send you an e-mail message between class sessions. This short exercise is simply to ensure that each student has some type of Internet access and can use e-mail on his or her own outside of the classroom.

Online Scavenger Hunt Have your students use at least three different search engines to find the answers to a series of questions. Indicate which search engine (and website) provided the answer to each question. This activity can also be performed in groups. If the class has library or Internet access, the groups can compete against each other. The group that answers all of the questions in the shortest amount of time is the winner. Sample questions: What is the average size and weight of a blue whale?; In what city was Edgar Allan Poe born?; Who is the CEO of General Electric?; What species of butterfly is the largest in the world?; Who was the eighteenth president of the United States?; What was the first college established in the United States?

Succeeding in Math and Science

Chapter 28: Mastering Math and Science

Math and science frighten many people. For those who have chosen to study in either of these fields in order to pursue a professional career this is probably not the case. But what about everyone else? More often than not, these others approach math and science courses with anxiety and fear, often avoiding such classes as long as possible even though they are requirements within their programs of study.

As a result of these feelings, these courses can become obstacles to academic success, instead of merely required courses to be completed successfully on the road to one's degree. In addition, mathematical concepts and the scientific method teach a process of thinking that can complement and improve critical thinking, problem solving, and decision-making.

Chapter 28 (along with Chapter 29) focuses on methods that students can use to approach math and science courses with confidence and to master the important academic skills that each subject has to offer students who are willing to accept the challenges presented by them.

This chapter will:

- advise students to choose math/science courses and their instructors carefully.
- remind students to consider such things as their present abilities, length of course and speed with which material is covered, instructor's style and methods, and course sequence when choosing math/science courses.
- teach students to be actively involved in their math/science classes.
- help to teach students how to use their textbooks to effectively support their course work.
- remind students that they must practice by solving problems in order to be successful in math/science courses.
- provide ideas and methods to help students solve problems more easily.
- introduce students to the scientific method and the importance of science in their daily lives.

Suggestions for Teaching

If you have chosen to cover Chapters 28 and 29, it is probably, in part, because many of your students are not majoring in math- or science-related areas. However, most other major subjects still require completion of math and/or science courses in their curricula. Since many students are intimidated by and anxious about these subjects, they can be obstacles, sometimes significant ones, to academic success.

Chapter 29 will focus specifically on math and science anxiety. This chapter (28) will first present methods and strategies by which students can approach these subjects in a more positive and less intimidating manner. Hopefully, these ideas and methods will help to make your students more successful.

Why are students so apprehensive about math and science? Often it is because of a lack of confidence in their abilities. They may not have performed well in these subject areas in the past. Therefore, they believe that they are not "good" at math and/or science and that they will not perform well in these subjects in the future. Students may also believe that as a result of their previous lack of success, they do not have the needed ability to be successful in science and math at the college level. Add to these views the fact that some students may have been away from school for many years before beginning or continuing college and therefore believe that they have forgotten whatever math and science knowledge they might have had long ago. As you might suspect, these students are setting themselves up for a self-fulfilling prophecy of limited success or even failure--a prediction that you must now help them to prove false.

First, you can attempt to make what many students consider abstract, complex, and strange subjects more common, real, and everyday. Show your students how math and the scientific method are often used in daily life. For example, students use some of these skills when they calculate the amount to leave for a tip in a restaurant, compare prices in a supermarket, research a paper for one of their courses, or try to repair a car. These situations are not uncommon or scary. In addition, remind your students that past difficulties do not necessarily indicate future struggles. They now have the opportunity to embrace the methods that you are about to teach them and approach their classes with a new attitude and improved ability.

Next, you should attempt to build confidence in your students and provide strategies by which they can more effectively approach these classes. Using Chapter 28 as a guide, set up methods and processes for your students to use in their math and science classes. Help them to create a methodology to use daily that builds a structure and plan into their study and course work. The *Guide* covers a series of topics that you can use to help your students in this way.

Before even enrolling in a math or science course, students should assess their present skill level carefully and choose an appropriate course and instructor. Students should take careful notes and review class and textbook material daily. They should practice solving problems often and over prepare. Remind your students that they should adapt their reading to this specific type of material and that they should read actively (see Chapter 9) and slowly. These are just some of the methods presented in this chapter to help build confidence in your students. Feel free to include your own ideas and methods here as well.

In order to develop and improve confidence, students should do two things. First, they should practice solving problems. The more easily one can construct and manipulate equations, understand logic, decipher word problems and questions, and determine what answer one is trying to solve, the more confident one becomes in his or her abilities. There is no substitute for practice. In fact, consider developing a set of simple mathematical questions and word problems, and occasionally give some of them to your students to solve. Practice will prove invaluable in the development of their skills.

Finally, remind your students that it is OK to get the wrong answer, especially in class. People learn from their mistakes. Fear of failure can paralyze people from ever taking a chance. That is, some students do not try to solve a problem because they are afraid that they will get the wrong answer. This is a major obstacle to learning in math and science courses. Therefore, you should try to help your students to be more comfortable with the wrong answers. I have found that if students are more comfortable with the belief that it is OK to be wrong some of the time, they are more likely to participate in class and, consequently, to become more active learners and to be more successful. This success then builds their confidence, which, in turn, makes them even more successful.

In order to create this cycle of success and confidence, it is important to help students to be more comfortable in their classroom and with each other. Consider using exercises or asking questions that many of your students will answer incorrectly. Ask a series of questions quickly so that each student will have an opportunity to be wrong. When almost everyone is wrong and sees there are no negative consequences, it is much easier to feel comfortable in one's lack of knowledge. Consequently, it is easier to participate. Try it and see how many more students are more actively a part of future classes. It will be a valuable skill that your students will be able to use in all of their classes, not only their math and science courses.

Additional Activities and Exercises

Math/Science Essay Have each student write a short (one-page) essay that details his or her history of success or failure in math and/or science. The essay should also include the reasons why he or she believes that he or she is intimidated by or afraid of math and/or science.

Common Uses Divide your students into groups. Have each group develop a list of ways in which people use math and/or science in their daily lives. Have each group read its list to the class. The group whose list has the greatest number of uses wins a prize. This exercise can also be used as a class discussion in which one large list is developed.

Help Resources Conduct a class discussion in which the students develop a list of all of the places and resources to which they could turn if they have trouble with math or science course work.

Let's Get It Wrong Develop a list of somewhat difficult math/science questions that you believe many (but not all) students will answer incorrectly. Ask each student a specific question. Ask all of the questions on the list in a continuous series. You can repeat questions with different students. The purpose of the exercise is to have students become more comfortable with giving the wrong answer in class.

Chapter 29: Reducing Math and Science Anxiety

A student's fear of poor performance or lack of confidence in his or her abilities in math and science often results in anxiety when confronted by these courses. Anxiety, stress, and fear often lead to poor class and test performance. A cycle develops that inhibits success in these areas.

Chapter 28 began to build a foundation for success in math and science courses. It developed strategies and methods for effective note-taking, problem-solving practice, review scheduling, active classroom participation, and effective test preparation. Chapter 29 addresses the next major obstacles to success in math and science: anxiety and apprehension.

This chapter will:

- help students to examine false assumptions that they might have about math and science.
- encourage students to assess their present level of ability in math and science in order to establish the correct starting point at which to begin taking these classes.
- help students to think positively about their abilities to achieve success in science and math.
- help students to take control of their math and science courses.
- provide ways to physically and mentally reduce stress and anxiety.
- encourage students to study with others and to create an environment in which it is OK to make mistakes.

Suggestions for Teaching

Anxiety about math and science is the result of a student's attitudes and feelings about these subjects and his or her belief in his or her ability (or inability) to master them. Therefore, in order to reduce or eliminate this anxiety, the student must confront, and possibly change, his or her attitudes and beliefs about these subjects and his or her abilities in them. Since your goal is to help your students to become successful, one of your tasks is to help them to manage this stress and anxiety.

You can begin by having your students realistically assess their abilities and skill levels in math and science in order to register for the proper courses. It makes no sense to enroll in a course for which one is not adequately prepared, since this greatly increases the possibility of poor performance. If a student decides that she is not prepared for a basic introductory course, she should consider extra preparation. She should first work to fill in any existing gaps in her math and science knowledge. Many colleges offer refresher or remedial courses, tutoring or extra help, or summer courses to help increase one's readiness in problem areas. Students should consider these options if needed in order to help build success and confidence, instead of finding oneself in a course beyond one's ability and struggling to overcome failure.

Next, remind your students not to underestimate the power of a positive attitude. There is great strength in believing in oneself and believing that one can be successful. Students should view science and math in college as a new beginning. They have new opportunities to succeed. Students need not be bound to previous mediocre performance. College provides new opportunities to write one's own history, as well as new resources and support systems to help achieve excellent performance. Students can take advantage of this. Students should believe that they will succeed!

Now it is time for students to actually do something. And that is practice. Nothing builds confidence and success like preparation. And preparation is built upon study and practice. Chapter 28 helped develop effective study habits and proper preparation, but one of the primary skills in math and science is problem solving. And there is really no other way to prepare for problems that one will encounter in class and on a test than to practice. Therefore, advise your students to solve many different kinds of problems as often as possible since one of the best ways to build success is to be prepared for any problem that one might find on an exam. So have them practice, practice, practice!

Finally, remember that anxiety is often manifested in physical symptoms such as a rapid heartbeat, excessive perspiration, difficulty breathing, as well as feelings of panic and the inability to remember what one has studied. It is also important to attend to these conditions since they too can be major obstacles to good grades. After all, math and science anxieties have been built up over many years. Several weeks of planning, preparation, and good study habits still may not be able to eliminate all of this accumulated stress and anxiety completely in the short term.

Remind your students to focus, relax, breathe deeply. Conduct a discussion that puts the math or science class into perspective in relation to a student's whole life plan. Remind them that even if the worse thing were to happen (a single failing grade on an exam), it would not end their college careers. Have your students focus on the planning and preparation that they have done, their positive and confident attitudes, and the belief that they can be successful. In conclusion, have them practice some deep, slow breathing techniques and exercises in class just in case all of the above fails and some students still experience distress and anxiety as they are about to start their exams.

Additional Activities and Exercises

Anxiety Triggers Divide your class into small groups. Have the group members discuss those things that make them nervous, intimidate them, or create anxiety about math or science for them. By the end of the discussion, each group should generate one list. Then the group should come up with one way to deal with each of the things or situations on the list. At the end of the exercise, each group should present its list, including the solutions, to the class.

Mock Quiz Create a short math or science test (one that will take about a half hour to complete). It does not have to cover any material that your students are studying. Administer it to your class. It will not count for any credit in any of the class members' classes. Have the students grade their tests when they have completed them. The object of this lesson is to remove some of the stress associated with math and science exams. Perhaps your students will be able to transfer the relaxed feeling that they had while taking this exam to their other science and math exams.

The Body Scan In order to practice relieving stress, have your students perform the checklist on page 196 of Chapter 17 ("Relax with a Body Scan"). Have students lie on the floor with an arm or book under their heads. If you prepare your students ahead of time, you can have them bring a small pillow into class. Students close their eyes and rest their attention on the soles of their feet. Notice and release any tension in that part of the body. Use the same "notice and release" techniques as students slowly move their attention through their calves, knees, thighs, pelvis, stomach, chest, shoulders, arms, neck, and head. After successfully completing this exercise, have your students take their seats.

Students should repeat the exercise at their seats so that they feel comfortable performing it when they encounter stress in a classroom situation.

Stress Relief Have your students perform the breathing exercises in the checklist found on page 186 in Chapter 16, "Sixty Seconds to Relaxation."

Exaggerate Your Fear Divide the class into small groups. Have each group take ten minutes to come up with the most outrageous and worst thing that will happen to them if they fail an exam. At the end of the exercise, have each group present its result to the class. Award a prize for the most outrageous result.

Let's Get It Wrong Develop a list of somewhat difficult math/science questions that you believe many (but not all) students will answer incorrectly. Ask each student a specific question. Ask all of the questions on the list in a continuous series. You can repeat questions with different students. The purpose of the exercise is to have students become more comfortable with giving the wrong answer in class.

I Can Do It Essay Have each student write a short (one-page) essay that details the ways in which he or she has been unsuccessful in his or her math/science classes in the past. The essay should also include the reasons why he or she believes that he or she is intimidated by or afraid of math and/or science. The paper should conclude with the steps that the student has taken or will take in order to reduce his or her anxiety and increase the chances of his or her success.

Chapter Quizzes

*Quizzes are also available to instructors online at http://masterstudent.college.hmco.com/instructors

Quiz – Chapter 1

1. During a student's first semester of college, he or she will probably
   a. not experience any stress.
   b. have more free time available than before starting school.
   c. have fewer exams than in high school.
   d. find that all instructors are understanding about balancing the demands of a job and schoolwork.

2. Which of the following behaviors can help new students to achieve academic success?
   a. Showing up for class
   b. Studying actively
   c. Learning to thrive with diversity
   d. All of the above

3. It is not OK for new students
   a. to feel anxious.
   b. to feel stress.
   c. to feel overwhelmed.
   d. to keep negative feelings repressed or hidden away.

4. A form of financial assistance that a student does not have to pay back is
   a. a federal student loan.
   b. a personal loan.
   c. a PLUS (Parent Loans for Undergraduate Students) loan.
   d. a Pell grant

5. A resumé
   a. should not list your education since you have not finished your degree.
   b. should not list awards.
   c. should not be started before your junior year of college.
   d. should be one page in length.

6. Many college professors
   a. took classes in how to teach.
   b. teach the same way.
   c. are very interested in research.
   d. speak at a very simple and basic level.

7. Good health
   a. has no influence on academic success.
   b. is something that busy students do not have time for.
   c. is one of the things that people must give up when they become students.
   d. can help people succeed in higher education.

8. Some stress
   a. can help a student stay alert and focused for an exam.
   b. is never a good thing.
   c. must always be eliminated right away.
   d. is the best reason to go to bed right away.

9. A student's first semester of college will probably be
   a. a time of no significant change from his or her previous lifestyle.
   b. a time of much failure.
   c. a time of no significant stress.
   d. a time of transition.

10. Students who successfully complete their first academic year of college
    a. will not encounter obstacles to their education after that.
    b. have a good chance of completing their degrees.
    c. often fail in their second academic year.
    d. often stop attending college and go to work full time.

Quiz – Chapter 2

1. Which of the following statements is true?
   a. All students process information and learn in the same way.
   b. Most professors teach in the same way.
   c. Students process information and learn in different ways.
   d. Most students fail courses because professors teach in ways that are contrary to the ways in which students process information.

2. How many modes of learning did Kolb identify in his Theory of Experiential Learning?
   a. 2
   b. 4
   c. 8
   d. 15

3. During the learning process, when a student applies ideas, tests theories, and uses knowledge to influence other people, it is called
   a. concrete experience.
   b. reflective observation.
   c. abstract conceptualization.
   d. active experimentation.

4. The best way to learn is
   a. through concrete experience.
   b. through abstract conceptualization.
   c. by the method or mode that works best for you.
   d. by using the four modes as a cycle and moving a learning situation through each of the four steps in some way.

5. In order to help students move the learning process through his cycle, Kolb proposes that students ask four questions in any learning situation. Which of the following is not one of those questions?
   a. Why?
   b. How?
   c. Where?
   d. What if?

6. When working in a group, it is best
   a. to try to get in a group where all the members share the same preferred learning style.
   b. to assess and accept the different learning styles of the members and then let each member participate using his or her strongest style or mode.
   c. to be the leader.
   d. to only do what is asked of you.

7. Students should
   a. accept everything that a professor says without question.
   b. demand that a professor change a grade when they disagree with her.
   c. take charge of their learning.
   d. not speak to their professor when they disagree with a grade that has been given, but go directly to the department chairperson and complain.

8. In Kolb's four modes of learning, the mode known as concrete experience could also be described as learning by
   a. feeling.
   b. watching.
   c. thinking.
   d. doing.

9. According to Chapter 2, discomfort
   a. is a natural part of the learning process.
   b. should be avoided at all costs when trying to learn something new.
   c. leads to stress and anxiety and, therefore, will only result in panic.
   d. tells the student that he should avoid trying something new.

10. Diversity, in both students and learning styles, occurs
    a. only in college classrooms.
    b. only in the workplace.
    c. in both college classrooms and the workplace.
    d. as a barrier to learning that usually cannot be overcome.

Quiz – Chapter 3

1. A panel organized by the American Philosophical Association concluded that critical thinkers have certain characteristics. Which of the following is not one of those characteristics?
   a. Quick to make decisions
   b. Truth-seeking
   c. Open mindedness
   d. Analytical

2. Critical thinking is least important in which of the following activities?
   a. Writing
   b. Reading
   c. Socializing
   d. Listening

3. Beliefs that guide our thinking and behavior are
   a. perceptions.
   b. attitudes.
   c. assumptions.
   d. logical.

4. A series of assertions that are clear, coherent, and consistent in terms of logical thought is
   a. an assumption.
   b. an argument.
   c. a proven fact.
   d. a falsehood.

5. A chain of logic that proceeds from specific to general
   a. can be thought of as deductive.
   b. is usually false.
   c. can be thought of as inductive.
   d. is the best way of thinking.

6. The best form of evidence to support an argument would be
   a. an opinion.
   b. expert testimony.
   c. a written statement.
   d. a hypothesis.

7. A skilled critical thinker recognizes that
   a. there is only one right answer.
   b. people who are right do not disagree.
   c. bias will never be present in formal writing.
   d. people disagree.

8. Terms with several different meanings are
   a. ambiguous.
   b. arguments.
   c. alliterative.
   d. analoguous.

9. When driving a car, the belief that other drivers know the meanings of traffic signals and signs is
   a. an argument.
   b. an attitude.
   c. an assumption.
   d. a mistake.

10. The function of an assertion is
   a. to state positively.
   b. to state negatively.
   c. to define a term or state a relationship between terms.
   d. to prove a point.

Quiz – Chapter 4

1. A technique for creating as many ideas as possible in a short time is
   a. enhancement.
   b. objectification.
   c. judgmentalism.
   d. brainstorming.

2. Journals
   a. must be formal and focused on a single topic to be effective.
   b. should be limited to one page per daily entry in order to maintain focus.
   c. can include entries about anything.
   d. rarely enhance creativity.

3. A happy and creative coincidence of ideas is known as
   a. brainstorming.
   b. a vacation.
   c. serendipity.
   d. a good time.

4. There is a follow-up step to creative thinking.
   a. It is where you rest.
   b. It is where you present your work.
   c. It is where you refine your ideas.
   d. It is where you try something new to enhance the creative process.

5. Creativity
   a. is only the province of artists, such as painters and novelists.
   b. is a process that you can consciously cultivate.
   c. is rarely used by people in the workplace.
   d. is not a process that you can consciously cultivate.

6. Which of the following statements about brainstorming is true?
   a. You should avoid making judgments or evaluating ideas during the brainstorming session.
   b. The best results are obtained when participants focus on multiple issues during a single brainstorming session.
   c. A time limit should never be set for a brainstorming session.
   d. Brainstorming is no longer very popular in the business world.

7. When one is trying to stimulate creativity, by asking questions on can generate
   a. more questions.
   b. new ideas.
   c. obstacles to creativity.
   d. silence.

8. Which of the following is not a way to stimulate creativity?
   a. Multiple-choice tests
   b. Keeping a journal
   c. Relaxation and reflection
   d. Exposure to many sources of new ideas

9. It is widely believed that sleep
   a. shuts down the creative process.
   b. does not help one to be a better problem solver.
   c. can help the creative process.
   d. can often help a student forget what he or she has studied.

10. When a brainstorming session is over
    a. always throw out the most unusual idea.
    b. never refine or discard any ideas.
    c. it is OK to discard some ideas, but only after you have considered and evaluated them.
    d. immediately choose some solution and move on to the next problem.

Quiz – Chapter 5

1. Your skills in thinking culminate in your ability
   a. to brainstorm.
   b. to pass a test.
   c. to think positively.
   d. to make decisions and solve problems.

2. The final step in making a decision should be
    a. a break.
    b. passivity.
    c. positivity.
    d. action.

3. Which of the following is not one of the steps in the decision-making process described by Engleberg and Wynn?
    a. Investigate
    b. Imagine
    c. Invigorate
    d. Insight

4. Problem solving
    a. can be thought of as less complex than decision making.
    b. exists at an even higher level of complexity than decision making.
    c. is the same as decision making.
    d. has nothing to do with decision making.

5. According to John Dewey, the first step in the problem-solving process is
    a. action.
    b. defining the problem.
    c. perceiving some felt difficulty.
    d. procrastination.

6. When working in a group, it is best
    a. to brainstorm right away.
    b. to spend only a short amount of time defining the problem since there are so many people participating.
    c. to establish constructive guidelines for working together at the beginning of the first meeting.
    d. to limit participation to those who have good ideas.

7. According to John Dewey, which of the following steps is not part of his problem- solving process?
    a. Positivity
    b. Performance
    c. Possibilities
    d. Problem

8. A method to sort and rank a large pool of ideas created by groups of people in meetings is called
    a. the Decreasing Options Technique.
    b. the Increasing Options Technique.
    c. the Expanding Options Technique.
    d. the Decreasing Availability Technique.

9. The phase of decision making that is concerned with generating as many options as possible, no matter how outlandish they first appear is the
    a. the Investigation phase.
    b. the Imagination phase.
    c. the Incubation phase.
    d. the Insight phase.

10. Decision making
    a. usually involves a series of questions.
    b. usually involves open-ended questions.
    c. usually comes down to a single question that can be answered by "yes" or "no."
    d. never involves questions that can be answered by "yes" or "no."

Quiz – Chapter 6

1. A life purpose
   a. should be direct and narrow.
   b. should be something that can be expected to be accomplished.
   c. should be something that will be finished by the time you are ready to retire.
   d. should be something that will not ever really be finished or attained.

2. The very first thing that one should do before learning effective time management skills is
   a. clear one week's activities from your calendar so that one can start fresh.
   b. set goals.
   c. determine a life purpose.
   d. brainstorm.

3. When creating a lifeline, the starting point
   a. is the present day.
   b. is the creator's birth date.
   c. is the date that the first goal will be completed.
   d. is the date of completion of the life purpose.

4. An effective goal statement is not
   a. concrete.
   b. concise.
   c. congruent with a life purpose.
   d. ambiguous.

5. Developing a life purpose and setting goals in turn helps one
   a. to set priorities that support the achievement of goals.
   b. to work less.
   c. to take on additional stress.
   d. to take fewer college courses.

6. If you believe that an activity in which you are participating is worth the time and effort that you are putting into it and it is satisfying, then
   a. you will make money by doing it well.
   b. it is consistent with your life purpose.
   c. it is serendipitous.
   d. it is inconsistent with your life purpose.

7. Goals
   a. will never be completed or accomplished.
   b. are items that can be put on a list and crossed off as you accomplish them.
   c. are not real because they are put on a list.
   d. should always be just out of reach.

8. When you have decided on a statement of life purpose
   a. you must not share it with anyone.
   b. you must write it down.
   c. you should never write it down.
   d. only share it with your life-purpose coach.

9. Getting an "A" on your next exam is
   a. a long-term goal.
   b. a mid-term goal.
   c. a short-term goal.
   d. impossible.

10. When creating a lifeline
   a. one must never estimate a date for one's death.
   b. one should include an estimated date of one's death.
   c. one should always use an end date one hundred years from the starting date.
   d. one should not include any new goals after the age of fifty.

Quiz – Chapter 7

1. Everyone gets to schedule
   a. 24 hours per week.
   b. 100 hours per week.
   c. 150 hours per week.
   d. 168 hours per week.

2. In time management, to discover how many hours you devote to each typical daily activity you should use
   a. a watch.
   b. a time monitor.
   c. a computer.
   d. a time restrictor.

3. The natural body clock that tells you when to sleep, get up, and so on, is also known as
   a. naturalistic time management.
   b. sleep rhythm management.
   c. circadian rhythm.
   d. rhythmic time management.

4. The ultimate benefit of monitoring and planning your time is
   a. balance.
   b. less free time.
   c. restrictions on activities.
   d. less time spent at work.

5. When studying, it is best
   a. to study wherever you can.
   b. to study whenever you can.
   c. to create a regular study place and time, if possible.
   d. to take time away from sleep in order to find more time to study.

6. Once you have created a to-do list or daily calendar, it is best
   a. to reorganize it.
   b. to prioritize it.
   c. to re-edit it.
   d. to put it away.

7. When creating a time monitor, which of the following activities should not be included?
   a. Sleeping
   b. Lunch
   c. A full-time job
   d. All activities should be included

8. Which of the following statements is true?
   a. Only well-organized people can learn how to manage their time well.
   b. Most people have little idea where their time really goes.
   c. A good breakfast will help you to be better organized throughout your day.
   d. Sports and leisure activities should be totally eliminated during the college semester.

9. The biggest obstacle to good time management is
   a. work.
   b. sports.
   c. procrastination.
   d. family.

10. When planning your weekly calendar, it is important to allow some time for
    a. stress.
    b. interruptions by family and friends.
    c. telephone time.
    d. fun.

Quiz – Chapter 8

1. One should choose a major
   a. early in one's college career.
   b. in one's first semester.
   c. in one's senior year of high school.
   d. after spending some time in college and after careful thought and consideration.

2. A skill is
   a. any activity that you improve with practice.
   b. always job related.
   c. something at which you become less proficient after you pass middle age.
   d. a natural talent.

3. General abilities that apply across many different content areas are
   a. content skills.
   b. transferable skills.
   c. general skills.
   d. educational skills.

4. A useful guide in choosing your major can be
   a. your friends.
   b. television.
   c. the most popular career choice at the present time.
   d. your life purpose.

5. The ability to speak Spanish is
   a. a content skill.
   b. a transferable skill.
   c. a general skill.
   d. an educational skill.

6. Many students
   a. refuse to change their majors.
   b. think that it is a sign of weakness to change their majors.
   c. change their majors before they graduate.
   d. do not know that they are allowed to change their majors.

7. A career choice
   a. is forever (it cannot be changed).
   b. should be considered carefully.
   c. should be an emotional decision.
   d. should involve the job at which you believe that you can earn the most money.

8. A career portfolio
   a. can only use work and projects from a student's senior year.
   b. should be started during a student's first year.
   c. should only include examples of content skills.
   d. is only appropriate for artistic students.

9. The core content, or "skeleton," of any job are
   a. tasks.
   b. skills.
   c. grades.
   d. plans.

10. Skill assessments, skill journals, and portfolios can be useful tools in the creation of
    a. a mind map.
    b. a brainstorm.
    c. a successful study group.
    d. a resumé.

Quiz – Chapter 9

1. It is important to read
   a. passively.
   b. persuasively.
   c. actively.
   d. actually.

2. A good way to determine what you are trying to get out of an assignment is to
   a. persuade somebody why you are reading.
   b. write a list of questions about the assignment.
   c. wait until after a class lecture to read the chapter that was covered.
   d. jump in and start reading without any preparation.

3. Before actually starting to read some material
   a. you should preview it.
   b. you should pick a specific time at which to end the reading session.
   c. you should find a reading partner.
   d. you should not undertake any preparation.

4. When reading a college textbook that you have purchased, you
   a. should never write in it.
   b. should only highlight it.
   c. should feel free to mark it up and write in it.
   d. should only write in the margins.

5. The final step in the active reading process is
   a. previewing.
   b. outlining.
   c. questioning.
   d. reflecting.

6. When previewing material, one should not look for
   a. anything that is underlined or printed in italics.
   b. visuals.
   c. a chapter summary.
   d. a shortcut.

7. Which of the following is not a step in the active reading process?
   a. Ask questions about what you read.
   b. Read to answer the questions.
   c. Reflect on the answers.
   d. Reword the questions as statements.

8. Reading textbooks should
   a. be done in one marathon session.
   b. not include any time for breaks.
   c. be done in short sessions, including breaks if needed.
   d. not ever include time for more than one break.

9. Which of the following statements is not true?
   a. Learning is born of questions.
   b. Questions distract you from your reading.
   c. Questions focus your attention and prompt you to become an active learner.
   d. Questions help you to get your money's worth from your textbooks.

10. Which of the following is not discussed as an important way to increase reading comprehension?
   a. Previewing
   b. Outlining
   c. Finding a reading buddy
   d. Reflecting on the material that you have read and the answers to the questions that you developed

Quiz – Chapter 10

1. The 80/20 rule states that
   a. only 80 percent of a class will show up to any given class session.
   b. only 20 percent of facts are statistically significant.
   c. 80 percent of the value created by any group derives from only 20 percent of its members.
   d. 80 percent of the time professors are right, and 20 percent of the time students are right.

2. Which of the following is not one of the steps in developing a reading plan?
   a. Estimate the total number of pages that you will need to read for each of your courses.
   b. Estimate how many pages you can read in each of your texts during one hour.
   c. Project the total number of hours you'll need to complete reading assignments in all of your courses.
   d. Determine which chapters to skip if the number of hours of reading that is required exceeds the number of hours that you have available.

3. Skillful readers
   a. determine their best reading rate and stick to it.
   b. speed up their reading rate to match the time available, regardless of the type of material that is being read.
   c. vary their reading rate according to the nature and purpose of the material.
   d. read as slowly as possible.

4. According to Adler and Van Doren, four questions can sum up the whole task of reading. Which of the following is not one of these questions?
   a. What is the book about as a whole?
   b. What is being said in detail?
   c. Where does it take place?
   d. Is it true?

5. A large vocabulary
   a. usually requires more effort than the benefit gained.
   b. gives more options for self-expression.
   c. rarely makes reading comprehension any easier.
   d. decreases the precision and power of your thinking by increasing your confusion.

6. A word's core meaning is found in
   a. its prefix.
   b. its root.
   c. its suffix.
   d. its anatomy.

7. The words and images that surround an unfamiliar word make up its
   a. construction.
   b. context.
   c. abstraction.
   d. direction.

8. The Internet has replaced
   a. the reading of books and magazines for most people.
   b. has borrowed its interface from books.
   c. has replaced textbooks for most students.
   d. has eliminated the need for reading in most cases.

9. Words with similar meaning are called
   a. synonyms.
   b. antonyms.
   c. oxymorons.
   d. similes.

10. In order to become a flexible reader,
   a. you must never stop to re-read part of a chapter that you have already read.
   b. you must never vary the pace of your reading.
   c. you should control and limit the content of what you read.
   d. you should adapt the pace of your reading according to the type of material being read and the purpose for which you are reading.

Quiz – Chapter 11

1. During four years of college, a good student will probably spend
   a. fifty hours taking notes.
   b. dozens of hours taking notes.
   c. hundreds of hours taking notes.
   d. very little time taking notes, since he or she is such a good student.

2. The note-taking process begins
   a. when you walk into the classroom.
   b. when you open your notebook.

c. when the professor starts to lecture.
d. well before you enter the classroom.

3. A personal digital assistant, such as a Palm Pilot,
   a. is too small to be used for taking notes.
   b. will not be able to store enough information to be used for note-taking.
   c. is not allowed to be brought in to many college classrooms.
   d. can be an effective way to take notes.

4. Note-taking while a professor lectures is dependent
   a. on how fast you can write.
   b. on how well you can listen.
   c. on whether you have eaten before attending class.
   d. on whether the class is held in the morning, afternoon, or evening.

5. The most important thing that a student should do before taking notes in a lecture
   a. is to eat something so that he or she is not hungry.
   b. is to greet the professor.
   c. is to complete the required reading.
   d. is to exercise so that you are awake and alert for the class.

6. If a professor speaks very quickly, a good way to slow him down is
   a. to complain.
   b. distract him by talking to a friend.
   c. ask a question.
   d. close your notebook and stop taking notes.

7. If you use a laptop computer to take notes, remember
   a. to connect to the Internet if possible so that you are in contact with friends during class.
   b. to bring a notebook and pen in case there is a computer problem during class.
   c. to bring copies of other assignments so you can complete other work when the professor repeats material.
   d. that you will not have to complete any required reading ahead of time, since this is the most effective method of note-taking.

8. When using abbreviations in note-taking,
   a. use only standard abbreviations.
   b. do not use vague abbreviations.
   c. never make up your own abbreviations.
   d. never combine words and numbers as abbreviations, such as "b4."

9. Your own ideas and opinions
   a. have no place in lecture notes.
   b. must be kept in the left margin.
   c. can be an effective way to help you remember key points and guide you in future studying.
   d. should only be put into your notes when you disagree with something that the professor says.

10. Which of the following is not one of the seven tools for powerful note-taking?
    a. Set the stage for note-taking.
    b. Prepare your instructor for note-taking.
    c. Choose your technology for note-taking.
    d. Predict test questions.

Quiz – Chapter 12

1. The Cornell Format of note-taking was developed
   a. by Walter Cornell.
   b. at Cornell University.
   c. specifically to be used on laptop computers.
   d. to focus on taking notes from textbooks.

2. In the Cornell Format, the two-inch space at the bottom of the page is
   a. the cue column.
   b. the summary area.
   c. the main note-taking area.
   d. the Cornell area.

3. When reading or listening to a lecture, *only* take notes in
   a. the cue column.
   b. the summary area.
   c. the large space in the right-hand side of the page.
   d. on a separate piece of paper.

4. One of the biggest advantages of the Cornell Format is
   a. its simplicity.
   b. its summary area.
   c. its complexity.
   d. its ability to slow down an instructor who speaks very quickly.

5. When using the Cornell Format, you must
   a. go back to your notes to fill in the cue column, which prompts review.
   b. wait a week before going back to complete your notes.
   c. rewrite your notes before you can use them to study.
   d. use a computer to gain the most benefit from the system.

6. The cue column in the Cornell Format can be
   a. difficult to learn, but it provides many benefits.
   b. a distraction.
   c. a great benefit when studying for an exam.
   d. easy to master, but it provides little benefit when studying.

7. One of the best uses of the summary area in the Cornell Format
   a. is to write down opinions of your instructor's teaching ability.
   b. is to remind yourself of the big picture or overall focus of the lecture or material.
   c. is to label and date your notes there.
   d. is to eliminate distractions by providing a place in which to write down unrelated ideas and thoughts.

8. When using the Cornell Format, the wide left-hand margin is called
   a. the cue column.
   b. the summary area.
   c. the main note-taking area.
   d. the Cornell area.

9. When taking notes during a lecture and using the Cornell Format
   a. you must use mind maps.
   b. you must use proper note-taking abbreviations.
   c. you must develop your own individual note-taking shorthand.
   d. you can use any particular format in this step.

10. Some students avoid the Cornell format because
    a. it is too complex.
    b. they do not like to hand-draw the lines to format their note pages.
    c. they believe that it is difficult because it comes from Cornell University.
    d. they believe that it is only useful for math and science courses.

Quiz – Chapter 13

1. Using maps for note-taking
   a. focuses on traditional note-taking skills.
   b. provides more structure than a method such as the Cornell Format.
   c. focuses on pattern-making and visuals.
   d. is a superior method for math and science courses.

2. Mind maps require
   a. structure and straight line connectors.
   b. more structure than note-taking in the Cornell Format.
   c. a computer to be an effective study aid.
   d. plenty of room.

3. When constructing a mind map, the main topic of a lecture should go
   a. at the top of the page.
   b. the center of the page.
   c. the top right-hand corner of the page.
   d. anywhere you want it.

4. Events that take place in chronological order can easily be represented
   a. on a mind map.
   b. on a time line.
   c. on a comparison chart.
   d. on a pie chart.

5. The main topic of a lecture
   a. should be smaller than the other headings on a mind map.
   b. should be circled or highlighted in some way.
   c. should always be written as a complete sentence.
   d. should be written in reverse.

6. A concept map
   a. is more formal than a mind map.
   b. is less formal than a mind map.
   c. is similar to traditional note-taking.
   d. looks like the Cornell Format when it is completed.

7. The important idea to keep in mind when creating a concept map
   a. is the strategic use of color.
   b. is its similarity to the Cornell Concept.
   c. is ultimately to arrange the concepts in a hierarchy.
   d. is the absence of color in its organization.

8. One of the advantages of studying from mind maps
   a. is the strategic use of color.
   b. is the ability to review maps more quickly than long passages of notes.
   c. is the ability to rewrite maps quickly.
   d. is the ability to convert notes from one map into the other.

9. Which of the following statements is true?
   a. All students prefer maps to traditional notes.
   b. Most students prefer mind maps to concept maps.
   c. Most students prefer concept maps to mind maps.
   d. Students who prefer much structure in their notes probably do not like mapping.

10. Mind maps
    a. can be used in conjunction with the Cornell Format.
    b. can never be used in conjunction with the Cornell Format.
    c. can only be placed into the summary section of notes taken using the Cornell Format.
    d. are clearly superior to notes taken in the Cornell Format.

Quiz – Chapter 14

1. Outlines
   a. must use Roman numerals.
   b. can be flexible and easy to use.
   c. must be rigid and complex.
   d. should not really be used for note-taking.

2. One of the key features of outlining is
   a. its Roman numerals.
   b. its easy conversion into a map.
   c. its replacement of the Cornell Format.
   d. its hierarchical structure.

3. When using an outline to take notes, it is important to
   a. focus on the type of headings that you will use.
   b. keep headings and levels relatively simple so you can focus on the material that you are trying to learn.
   c. always use complete sentences for headings.
   d. memorize the system of Roman numerals.

4. When creating an outline of quick reminders, you should use
   a. a traditional outline format.
   b. a topic outline.
   c. a sentence outline.
   d. your daily planner.

5. Computers
   a. do not enhance the outlining process.
   b. should not be used for outlining.
   c. often have word-processing features that allow you to easily use and enhance the outlining process.
   d. are only effective for creating traditional outlines.

6. Which of the following would *not* be an advantage of sentence outlines?
   a. Great clarity and precision about what was heard or read
   b. Large amount of content is captured
   c. Brief and quick
   d. Can be converted easily into an essay

7. Which of the following is the most effective aid to studying?
   a. Mind mapping
   b. Content mapping
   c. Outlining
   d. It depends on the preference and skill of the student

8. Outline headings generally move from
   a. general to specific.
   b. specific to general.
   c. out from the center of the page.
   d. from the outside of the page in toward the center of the page.

9. Outlining is appropriate for
   a. note-taking.
   b. studying.
   c. organizing writing assignments.
   d. all of the above.

10. Which of the following is *not* appropriate for outline headings?
   a. Roman numerals.
   b. All-capital letters.
   c. Indenting new levels of headings.
   d. Any method that differentiates levels of headings is appropriate.

Quiz – Chapter 15

1. The first step in revising notes is
   a. to clean them up.
   b. to recreate them.
   c. to put them away safely until it is time to study for an exam.
   d. to put them into a journal.

2. The goal of taking notes is
   a. to act like a real college student.
   b. to condense a lecture to its most important points.
   c. to reflect on the subject matter and bring it into clear focus and understanding.
   d. pointless for most students.

3. Notes should be reviewed
   a. the day before an exam.
   b. immediately before an exam.
   c. regularly.
   d. according to a random schedule to achieve maximum reinforcement.

4. The two types of notes that a student can take when reading are
   a. review and revision.
   b. research and revision.
   c. review and research.
   d. retrospective and revision.

5. Notes that are condensed, updated, refined, and reorganized
   a. create a lot of work for students.
   b. add value to the notes.
   c. confuse students.
   d. create disorganized study aids.

6. According to Dave Ellis, when writing in a journal, statements of commitment to take a certain action are
   a. Discovery Statements.
   b. Intention Statements.
   c. rarely acted upon.
   d. not appropriate journal topics.

7. Notes should
   a. be as brief as possible.
   b. help a student to study for an exam.
   c. only be reviewed twenty-four hours (or longer) after a class has ended.
   d. be the only source of material that a student uses to study for an exam.

8. Notes that you make in order to write papers and prepare for presentations are
   a. review notes.
   b. research notes.
   c. retrospective notes.
   d. Cornell notes.

9. A journal should not be used to
   a. promote insight and change.
   b. manage stress.
   c. practice writing skills.
   d. impress an instructor.

10. In order to take more effective notes
    a. condense a passage to key quotations.
    b. write smaller.
    c. do not use a variety of formats.
    d. do not revise notes after a class has ended.

Quiz – Chapter 16

1. A process that people use to create mental images of past events is one of the definitions of
   a. learning.
   b. college success.
   c. memory.
   d. the brain.

2. Marathon study sessions
   a. benefit memory.
   b. are effective study methods.
   c. do not help the memory process.
   d. are more effective than many short study sessions.

3. One of the easiest and best relaxation techniques is through
   a. sleep.
   b. breathing.
   c. memorization.
   d. mnemonics.

4. Which of the following is not one of the memory "gates" explained in Chapter 16?
   a. short-term memory.
   b. mid-term memory.
   c. long-term memory.
   d. sensory memory.

5. The process of consciously encoding information is called
   a. elastication.
   b. enforcement.
   c. elaboration.
   d. corroboration.

6. One of the most effective memory aids is the creation of
   a. assimilations.
   b. elaborations.
   c. associations.
   d. evaluations.

7. The most common and easily used memory device is
   a. refinement.
   b. elaboration.
   c. mnemonics.
   d. repetition.

8. The *Master Student Guide to Academic Success* lists seven steps to remembering. The first one is
   a. rephrase.
   b. recite.
   c. reduce.
   d. relax.

9. A common form of verbal association that can be an effective memory device is
   a. refinement.
   b. elaboration.
   c. mnemonics.
   d. repetition.

10. Stress
    a. often interferes with memory.
    b. usually helps one to study more efficiently.
    c. is easily eliminated.
    d. does not usually interfere with memory.

Quiz – Chapter 17

1. Which of the following promotes memory recall?
   a. Stress
   b. Relaxation
   c. Marathon study sessions
   d. Fear of failure

2. Which of the following is not a mnemonic memory recall device?
   a. Acrostics
   b. Acronyms
   c. Assimilations
   d. Rhymes

3. When the answer is on the tip of your tongue but you cannot recall it, you should
   a. give up and move on.
   b. be patient and calmly wait it out.
   c. panic.
   d. hand in the test immediately.

4. Which of the following is not one of the eight ways to enhance recall as listed in Chapter 17 of the *Master Student Guide*?
   a. Write an essay.
   b. Focus your attention and relax.
   c. Use mnemonic devices.
   d. Recreate the original context.

5. Items in short-term memory tend to fade
   a. in a few hours.
   b. in one day.
   c. after several days.
   d. in about a week.

6. Notes
   a. should first be reviewed within twenty-four hours.
   b. should be reviewed often.
   c. should be reviewed actively.
   d. should be reviewed once before an exam.

7. One of the best ways to relax to relieve stress while taking an exam is
   a. to take a nap.
   b. to lie on the floor and breathe.
   c. to practice special breathing techniques.
   d. to have a snack.

8. When you try to recall information by remembering the location in which you studied the information and what was going on when you studied it, you are
   a. assimilating the knowledge.
   b. recreating the original context.
   c. studying mnemonically.
   d. panicking.

9. How quickly should one review new material?
   a. Within twenty-four hours
   b. Sometime within a week of the lecture
   c. Whenever you get to it, as long as you review it at least twice before the exam
   d. The night before the exam for maximum retention

10. One of the most effective places in which to study for an exam is
    a. your bedroom.
    b. the cafeteria of your dormitory.
    c. outside.
    d. in the room in which the exam will be given.

Quiz – Chapter 18

1. One of the best ways to begin preparations for an exam
   a. is to review your notes.
   b. is to form a study group.
   c. is to create a study checklist.
   d. is to get enough sleep the night before an exam.

2. Review for an exam should
   a. begin two weeks prior to the scheduled date of the exam.
   b. begin one week prior to the scheduled date of the exam.
   c. begin two days before the scheduled date of the exam.
   d. occur regularly and early.

3. Study groups
   a. should contain no more than three people.
   b. are one of the least effective study methods.
   c. should only be used for the most difficult subjects.
   d. can be an effective way to study for tests.

4. A study checklist
   a. is the most effective type of review sheet.
   b. is a type of to-do list.
   c. can only contain lists of notes to be studied.
   d. is the last thing that one should do to prepare for an exam.

5. Which of the following statements is false?
   a. Successful and well-prepared students never feel test anxiety.
   b. Some nervousness related to testing can be a good thing.
   c. Test anxiety is not inevitable
   d. Resisting feelings of test anxiety is not the best way of dealing with them.

6. It is recommended that a student should review each subject
   a. at least once each day.
   b. at least once each week.
   c. at least once each day the week before an exam.
   d. several days before an exam.

7. Summary notes
   a. contain all your lecture notes rewritten in an organized form.
   b. are materials that you create specifically to review for tests.
   c. is another name for notes in the Cornell Format.
   d. are notes that have been taken for a research paper or project.

8. Which of the following would not be an effective way to study for an exam?
   a. Using flash cards.
   b. Creating a mock test.
   c. Stealing copies of previous tests.
   d. Creating summary notes.

9. Which is of the following is not an activity that you would probably use in a study group?
   a. Brainstorming test questions.
   b. Teaching each other.
   c. Creating large mind maps from the members' combined notes.
   d. Reading new material.

10. Which of the following would not be a good way to reduce test anxiety?
    a. Put tests and grades in perspective.
    b. Over prepare.
    c. Study all night before an exam.
    d. Practice controlled breathing techniques.

Quiz – Chapter 19

1. Before answering any questions on an exam
   a. you should have something to eat.
   b. you should take a break.
   c. you should plan your test-taking strategy.
   d. you should ask your instructor how much time you have to complete the test.

2. As soon as the test is handed out
   a. close your eyes and pray.
   b. create a pleasant visual image in your mind.
   c. write down any key information or formulas that you are sure will be on the exam.
   d. answer the first question before you forget something.

3. When taking an exam, most people recommend that you
   a. answer the multiple-choice questions first.
   b. answer the essay questions first.
   c. answer the shortest, easiest questions first.
   d. answer the questions at the back of the exam first to reduce stress.

4. Which of the following ideas is not an effective method to use if you get stuck on a test question?
   a. Look for answers in other test questions.
   b. Skip it for now.
   c. Free write.
   d. Leave it blank and hope that it's not worth very many points.

5. Grading essay questions is a somewhat subjective process, therefore
   a. try to be vague so the instructor won't realize that you don't know what you're talking about.
   b. write neatly so the instructor can read what you are writing.
   c. write a lot of information so the instructor will eventually get tired of reading it.
   d. write illegibly so the instructor will feel sorry for you.

6. Open-book tests
   a. are usually more difficult than standard exams.
   b. are usually easier than standard exams.
   c. do not require much review.
   d. are preferable to standard exams.

7. Scanning the entire test before starting is also known as
   a. test reconciliation.
   b. test reconnaissance.
   c. summary notation.
   d. test encoding.

8. Usually, the test questions that are worth the greatest number of points are
   a. true/false questions.
   b. multiple-choice questions.
   c. matching questions.
   d. essay questions.

9. Taking a test
   a. is much different than studying for a test.
   b. should be no different than studying for a test.
   c. is one of the least stressful experiences that a student will encounter.
   d. should be avoided at all costs.

10. When taking an exam, essay questions should be done
    a. first.
    b. last.
    c. as quickly as possible.
    d. it depends on several factors.

Quiz – Chapter 20

1. Research that is described as thorough
    a. will include the exact information that will be needed for a paper.
    b. will include more information than you can include in your final paper.
    c. will include just the amount of information needed for your paper so you do not waste any time.
    d. will take at least a month to find.

2. Which of the following is not a technique that should be used to find a topic about which to write?
    a. Brainstorming.
    b. Free writing.
    c. Charades.
    d. Mind mapping.

3. One should avoid topics that are
    a. too broad.
    b. too narrow.
    c. too boring.
    d. all of the above.

4. A concise sentence that clearly summarizes what you want to say in your paper is called
    a. an outline sentence.
    b. a leading sentence.
    c. a thesis statement.
    d. an assertion statement.

5. If you are trying to change the way someone acts, then you are trying to create
    a. a cognitive change.
    b. an affective change.
    c. a behavioral change.
    d. an academic change.

6. Before writing, you should
    a. clear your mind.
    b. get a good night's sleep.
    c. clean your room to create a neat environment.
    d. research.

7. When brainstorming topics for a paper,
    a. you must perform this activity alone.
    b. you should use a computer.
    c. you can perform this activity with others.
    d. you should write in many colors to enhance creativity.

8. You probably selected an appropriate topic if you can explain it to someone
    a. in fifteen seconds.
    b. in sixty seconds.
    c. in two minutes.
    d. in five minutes.

9. When free writing, you should continue writing
   a. until you are exhausted.
   b. until you can't think of anything else to write about.
   c. until someone comes in and interrupts you.
   d. for a set period of time.

10. A thesis statement
    a. should not be changed after it is written down.
    b. can be flexible.
    c. should be indefinite.
    d. should be vague.

Quiz – Chapter 21

1. First-hand original research materials are known as
   a. primary sources.
   b. secondary sources.
   c. library sources.
   d. Internet sources.

2. If you have not used a library to conduct much research in the past, you should start with
   a. the Internet.
   b. the card catalog.
   c. the librarian.
   d. microfilm.

3. When using search engines on the Internet, you look for material on your topic by using
   a. locks.
   b. doorways.
   c. key words.
   d. motor words.

4. The formal listing of the sources that you use as research in your paper is called
   a. the biography.
   b. the bibliography.
   c. the index.
   d. the identification log.

5. Using your own words and sentence structure while using another person's ideas is called
   a. paraphrasing.
   b. plagiarism.
   c. stealing.
   d. illegal.

6. Interviewing an expert source is a form of
   a. primary research.
   b. secondary research.
   c. plagiaristic research.
   d. fun research.

7. After finding a possible source, you should
   a. refer it to your professor for review.
   b. evaluate it.
   c. print it out or copy it.
   d. delete it so that none of your classmates can use the same source in their papers.

8. Population statistics can often be found in
   a. indexes.
   b. almanacs.
   c. periodicals.
   d. scholarly journals.

9. Magazine articles are usually classified as
   a. primary sources.
   b. secondary sources.
   c. insufficient sources.
   d. subordinate sources.

10. Research is less useful if it is
    a. done by the government.
    b. biased.
    c. done by a student.
    d. found on the Internet.

Quiz – Chapter 22

1. Which of the following is not one of the three steps of the writing process as explained in Chapter 22 of the *Master Student Guide*?
   a. Prewriting
   b. Writing
   c. Revising
   d. Mapping

2. An outline
   a. can keep you focused and provide structure.
   b. can force you to write.
   c. prevents you from creating a map.
   d. is a substitute for a writing plan.

3. An introduction
   a. must always be written first.
   b. must always be written last.
   c. should not contain the thesis statement.
   d. should introduce your audience to what you are writing about and grab their attention.

4. Before writing or prewriting, you should
   a. set up a writing map.
   b. set up a writing schedule.
   c. set up an outline.
   d. get some help.

5. Writing can often be considered as a series of steps, and
   a. there is a specific order that must be followed.
   b. they must be completed consecutively in a single writing session for best results.
   c. it is a personal process in which the order can be adapted by each writer.
   d. each one will normally take at least a day to complete.

6. Writing that is done in groups is also called
   a. group development.
   b. multiple authoring.
   c. collaborative writing.
   d. creative enhancement.

7. Which of the following activities is not part of the prewriting process?
   a. Creating a thesis statement
   b. Completing a first draft
   c. Outlining
   d. Researching

8. When developing a writing schedule, you should estimate the total length of time that the project will take to complete and
   a. then cut this time in half.
   b. double it.
   c. triple it.
   d. stick to this estimate no matter what.

9. The most basic organizing pattern for your writing is
   a. introduction, body, conclusion.
   b. thesis statement, introduction, conclusion.
   c. introduction, thesis statement, conclusion.
   d. summary, thesis statement, conclusion.

10. Collaborative writing
    a. is more effective than writing alone.
    b. is quicker than writing alone.
    c. allows the writers to complete a project using only a single draft.
    d. can be a source of conflict in the writing process.

Quiz – Chapter 23

1. The best way to develop skill in writing is by
   a. studying.
   b. reviewing your notes.
   c. practicing.
   d. editing.

2. In free writing
   a. keep your hands moving.
   b. don't think.
   c. don't stop.
   d. all of the above.

3. Write a first draft
   a. with care.
   b. slowly.
   c. quickly.
   d. before you write your outline.

4. When you have finished your first draft,
   a. revise it immediately.
   b. edit it immediately.
   c. transform it into an outline.
   d. put it aside for a while.

5. Sometimes the hardest part of writing a first draft is
   a. getting started.
   b. stopping.
   c. editing while you write.
   d. getting rid of anxiety.

6. For free writing,
   a. you can use a computer.
   b. never use a computer.
   c. you must write in a classroom.
   d. you should not use a journal.

7. Which of the following is not a good way to practice writing?
   a. Write letters
   b. Write in a journal
   c. Free writing on a computer
   d. Writing only when you are required to do so

8. If you have created a formal sentence outline,
   a. it will be harder to write your first draft.
   b. you have the basic structure of your first draft in place.
   c. you will not be able to write your first draft.
   d. you should edit the outline before writing your first draft.

9. After you complete your second and third drafts,
   a. get rid of the first draft.
   b. save your first draft.
   c. save only the last draft that you have completed.
   d. combine all of your drafts.

10. A first draft will look good to you
   a. and your instructor.
   b. and the person editing it.
   c. but may still have grammatical errors.
   d. and everyone else.

Quiz – Chapter 24

1. How many drafts should be written for any college-level writing assignment?
   a. One
   b. Two
   c. Three
   d. As many as it takes to produce an assignment of high quality

2. Ernest Hemingway rewrote the last page of *A Farewell to Arms* how many times?
   a. Two times
   b. Three times
   c. Twelve times
   d. Thirty-nine times

3. People who rewrite
   a. follow instructions.
   b. care.
   c. are neurotic.
   d. spend too much time on their writing and not enough time on their other course work.

4. When rewriting a draft, one should
   a. slow down.
   b. complete it as quickly as possible.
   c. be sure that no one else looks at it.
   d. leave no time between revising the first and second drafts.

5. The best person from whom to get feedback about your writing is
   a. a professor.
   b. your friends.
   c. your parents.
   d. anyone who will take the time to carefully review your writing.

6. When giving feedback about someone else's writing,
   a. be sure to do it quickly.
   b. do it constructively.
   c. give it honestly and tactlessly.
   d. do not point out all of the errors because this will hurt the writer's feelings.

7. Using lots of adjectives and adverbs
   a. creates a very descriptive paper.
   b. adds unnecessary bulk to your writing and weakens your message.
   c. will produce an essay of high quality.
   d. in your first draft reduces the need for a second draft.

8. Consider a long sentence one that has more than
   a. twelve words.
   b. twenty-five words.
   c. fifty words.
   d. one hundred words.

9. Whenever possible, write
   a. in the active voice.
   b. in the passive voice.
   c. in your own personal voice.
   d. in clothes you are comfortable in.

10. Who is ultimately responsible for revising your writing?
    a. The person providing feedback on your first draft
    b. Your professor
    c. Your editor
    d. The writer (you)

Quiz – Chapter 25

1. A presentation includes
   a. public speaking.
   b. handout materials.
   c. visual elements.
   d. listening to a group make a presentation.

2. Your presentation
   a. should have a thesis statement.
   b. does not need a thesis statement.
   c. should have a hidden thesis statement.
   d. should have a written thesis statement.

3. When preparing a speech, you should
   a. harass your audience.
   b. soothe your audience.
   c. analyze your audience.
   d. ignore your audience.

4. When using index cards as notes for a presentation, you should number them
   a. so that you will know how long you are speaking.
   b. so that you can put them back in order if you drop them.
   c. so that someone can return them if you lose them.
   d. so that the audience will know the order of your speech.

5. The most important part of a speech is probably
   a. the beginning.
   b. the middle.
   c. the end.
   d. the part right before the audience falls asleep.

6. You should rehearse your speech or presentation
   a. once.
   b. twice.
   c. until you feel comfortable with it.
   d. until you have memorized it.

7. It is normal
   a. to do better on a group presentation than on an individual presentation.
   b. to feel nervous before making a presentation.
   c. to faint while giving a speech.
   d. to refuse to make a presentation.

8. The introduction of a speech is so important because
   a. it is where you introduce yourself.
   b. it is where you grab the audience's attention.
   c. it is where the audience will decide if they are going to sleep or not.
   d. it is where you analyze the audience.

9. When creating a PowerPoint presentation, you should *not*
   a. use simple text.
   b. proofread.
   c. rehearse the timing of the slides.
   d. use as many colors as possible.

10. A powerful strategy for reducing anxiety before and during a presentation is
    a. to cry right before you give your speech.
    b. to prepare thoroughly.
    c. to panic.
    d. to ask someone else to deliver your speech.

Quiz – Chapter 26

1. A student attending college
   a. should bring his or her own computer to campus.
   b. should not bring his or her own computer to campus.
   c. should make the college supply him with a laptop computer.
   d. should evaluate the computer resources available at the college and his or her needs and decide whether he or she needs to bring his or her own computer to campus

2. When creating or editing a computer file, you should save your work
   a. every minute.
   b. every five minutes.
   c. once an hour.
   d. once during the work session.

3. If you have decided to bring a computer on to campus, it is best to bring
   a. a laptop.
   b. a desktop.
   c. a personal digital assistant.
   d. the type of computer that best meets your needs.

4. Space on a computer's hard drive is measured in
   a. megahertz.
   b. gigabytes.
   c. megabits.
   d. TCP/IP.

5. Information technology
   a. can be integrated into a student's daily study tasks.
   b. cannot be integrated into a student's daily study tasks.
   c. can be integrated into a student's daily study tasks but it is very difficult to do so.
   d. should not be integrated into daily study tasks because the effort required to do so is much greater than the small benefit that is gained by studying this way.

6. In order to protect your work, you should
   a. create a backup copy of your file on separate storage media.
   b. never create a backup file.
   c. not create backup files because other students will then be able to steal your ideas.
   d. create backup copies of your important files and give them to a friend to keep safe.

7. Most colleges
   a. provide computers for a student's personal use.
   b. provide student access to computers in many places throughout the campus.
   c. require students to buy their own computers.
   d. prohibit students from bringing laptop computers into the classroom.

8. Another name for a network adapter or network Internet card is
   a. a gigabyte card.
   b. a RAM card.
   c. an Ethernet card.
   d. a megahertz card.

9. A device that allows you to read and write data to CDs and DVDs is called
   a. a RAM reader.
   b. an Ethernet card.
   c. an optical drive.
   d. a Zip drive.

10. A laptop computer
    a. can be an effective way to take notes in a classroom.
    b. should not be used to take notes in a classroom.
    c. is usually not allowed to be brought into the classroom.
    d. is often a major distraction to the student using it for taking notes in the classroom and to those around him.

Quiz – Chapter 27

1. The online community refers to
   a. telephone conference calls.
   b. Internet communities.
   c. a secret society.
   d. an academic Internet group.

2. People read
   a. more slowly on a computer screen than on paper.
   b. more quickly on a computer screen than on paper.
   c. at about the same rate on a computer screen as on paper.
   d. carelessly on both the computer screen and on paper.

3. E-mail addresses for groups of people who want to automatically receive messages on a certain topic are called
   a. chat rooms.
   b. e-mail lists.
   c. instant messages.
   d. search engines.

4. Which of the following is not a search engine?
   a. www.google.com
   b. www.altavista.com
   c. www.robby.com
   d. www.yahoo.com

5. Internet etiquette is also called
   a. e-mailetiquette.
   b. message-tiquette.
   c. netiquette.
   d. connect-etiquette.

6. When teachers and learners are separated geographically but communicate by the Internet or other technology to conduct the learning process, it is called
   a. Internet learning.
   b. technology learning.
   c. computer learning.
   d. distance learning.

7. When writing an e-mail message, it is best
   a. to write a few long sentences.
   b. to use long line lengths so you use as few lines as possible.
   c. to write short sentences.
   d. to use all capital letters.

8. The acronym 218 in an e-mail message means
   a. 8:21.
   b. too late.
   c. two late.
   d. two-hundred-eighteen.

9. When sending an e-mail message, a long document should be
   a. embedded in the e-mail.
   b. avoided at all costs.
   c. sent as an attached document.
   d. bounced over to the recipient.

10. E-mail messages cannot convey
   a. humor.
   b. information.
   c. tone and sarcasm.
   d. attachments.

Quiz – Chapter 28

1. Math and science
   a. are the most important subjects that one can study in college.
   b. can teach a process of thinking that is valuable in itself.
   c. are the most difficult subjects in college.
   d. are the scariest subjects in college.

2. Success in math starts
   a. before you set foot in a classroom.
   b. as soon as you set foot in the classroom.
   c. when the professor starts lecturing.
   d. when you take the first test.

3. A student should review his or her work in math or science
   a. daily.
   b. twice per week.
   c. once per week.
   d. during the week preceding an exam.

4. When a math course relies extensively on the use of a calculator,
   a. this is a bad omen.
   b. you should drop the course immediately.
   c. you should buy the best calculator that you can find.
   d. you should create a section in your notebook to record keystroke sequences for key formulas.

5. If you find that you are confused in a math or science course, you should
   a. not admit it and try and figure things out before the test.
   b. ask for help right away.
   c. try to figure thing out before the test and if you cannot, then ask for help the week before the exam is scheduled.
   d. drop the course right away.

6. When reading a math or science textbook, it is especially important to
   a. read quickly.
   b. skim through the formulas and examples.
   c. read actively.
   d. disregard most of the text and rely on the instructor and friends for explanations.

7. When trying to solve a mathematical equation,
   a. you want to try and group all of the unknowns on one side of the equation.
   b. reduce the number of unknowns as much as possible.
   c. maximize the number of unknowns.
   d. increase the number of variables present in the equation.

8. An error that you make when you do not understand or know which principle or rule to use when solving a math problem is
   a. a concept error.
   b. an application error.
   c. a careless error.
   d. a mathematical mistake.

9. The first major step in the scientific method is
   a. making your findings public.
   b. analyzing data.
   c. designing test experiences.
   d. creating a hypothesis.

10. One of the additional elements of science classes that are not usually found in other types of classes
    a. is reflection time.
    b. are lab sessions.
    c. is independent study time.
    d. is journal writing.

Quiz – Chapter 29

1. Succeeding in math and science
   a. can help you to achieve academic success.
   b. can turn you into a nerd.
   c. can cause anxiety and stress.
   d. can cause your friends to stay away from you.

2. The fields of math and science
   a. have no room for imagination.
   b. allow only white males to be successful in them.
   c. leave no room for creativity.
   d. value creativity and imagination.

3. When concepts tend to build upon each other in sequential order, a subject is said to be
   a. creative.
   b. participatory.
   c. cumulative.
   d. proficient.

4. Anxiety
   a. is only a mental state or condition.
   b. does not result from the fear of math or science.
   c. can have physical symptoms.
   d. must be eliminated before one can take a test.

5. Cooperative learning refers to
   a. learning by oneself.
   b. learning with the instructor.
   c. learning with others.
   d. learning with the help of a computer.

6. When registering for a math or science course, choose the one
   a. that is below your present level of proficiency (so that you can earn a good grade).
   b. that is consistent with your current level of proficiency.
   c. that is beyond your current level of proficiency.
   d. that has a name that you like.

7. When a student repeatedly says that he or she will not do well in math or science and then does not perform well on exams, it is called
   a. a tragedy.
   b. a self-fulfilling prophecy.
   c. a mistake.
   d. an anxious inconsistency.

8. When you feel anxious about a course such as math or science, you should
   a. repress these feelings.
   b. ignore these feelings.
   c. allow these feeling to come to the surface.
   d. ask the instructor if you can take the exam later.

9. Which of the following statements is false?
   a. Many students experience math and/or science anxiety.
   b. Many students succeed at math and science.
   c. Deep breathing can help remove feelings of stress.
   d. Only some people succeed at math and science.

10. Most college programs
    a. do not include math and science courses.
    b. require math and science courses.
    c. allow students to avoid math and science course in certain circumstances.
    d. only require the most advanced students to take math and science courses.

Answers – Chapter Quizzes

Chapter 1	Chapter 2	Chapter 3	Chapter 4	Chapter 5
1. c	1. c	1. a	1. d	1. d
2. d	2. b	2. c	2. c	2. d
3. d	3. d	3. c	3. c	3. c
4. d	4. d	4. b	4. c	4. b
5. d	5. c	5. c	5. b	5. c
6. d	6. b	6. b	6. a	6. c
7. d	7. c	7. d	7. b	7. a
8. a	8. a	8. a	8. a	8. a
9. d	9. a	9. c	9. c	9. b
10. b	10. c	10. c	10. c	10. c
Chapter 6	**Chapter 7**	**Chapter 8**	**Chapter 9**	**Chapter 10**
1. d	1. d	1. d	1. c	1. c
2. c	2. b	2. a	2. b	2. d
3. b	3. c	3. b	3. a	3. c
4. d	4. a	4. d	4. c	4. c
5. a	5. c	5. a	5. d	5. b
6. b	6. b	6. c	6. d	6. b
7. b	7. d	7. b	7. d	7. b
8. b	8. b	8. b	8. c	8. b
9. c	9. c	9. b	9. b	9. a
10. b	10. d	10. d	10. c	10. d
Chapter 11	**Chapter 12**	**Chapter 13**	**Chapter 14**	**Chapter 15**
1. c	1. b	1. c	1. b	1. a
2. d	2. b	2. d	2. d	2. b
3. d	3. c	3. b	3. b	3. c
4. b	4. a	4. b	4. b	4. c
5. c	5. a	5. b	5. c	5. b
6. c	6. c	6. a	6. c	6. b
7. b	7. b	7. c	7. d	7. b
8. b	8. a	8. b	8. a	8. b
9. c	9. d	9. d	9. d	9. d
10. b	10. b	10. a	10. d	10. a

Chapter 16	**Chapter 17**	**Chapter 18**	**Chapter 19**	**Chapter 20**
1. c	**1. b**	**1. c**	**1. c**	**1. b**
2. c	**2. c**	**2. d**	**2. c**	**2. c**
3. b	**3. b**	**3. d**	**3. c**	**3. d**
4. b	**4. a**	**4. b**	**4. d**	**4. c**
5. c	**5. a**	**5. b**	**5. b**	**5. c**
6. c	**6. a**	**6. b**	**6. a**	**6. d**
7. d	**7. c**	**7. b**	**7. b**	**7. c**
8. d	**8. b**	**8. c**	**8. d**	**8. a**
9. c	**9. a**	**9. d**	**9. a**	**9. d**
10. a	**10. d**	**10. c**	**10. b**	**10. b**
Chapter 21	**Chapter 22**	**Chapter 23**	**Chapter 24**	**Chapter 25**
1. a	**1. d**	**1. c**	**1. d**	**1. d**
2. c	**2. a**	**2. d**	**2. d**	**2. a**
3. c	**3. d**	**3. c**	**3. b**	**3. c**
4. b	**4. b**	**4. d**	**4. a**	**4. b**
5. a	**5. c**	**5. a**	**5. d**	**5. a**
6. a	**6. c**	**6. b**	**6. b**	**6. c**
7. b	**7. b**	**7. d**	**7. b**	**7. b**
8. a	**8. b**	**8. b**	**8. b**	**8. b**
9. b	**9. a**	**9. b**	**9. a**	**9. d**
10. b	**10. d**	**10. c**	**10. d**	**10. b**
Chapter 26	**Chapter 27**	**Chapter 28**	**Chapter 29**	
1. d	**1. b**	**1. b**	**1. a**	
2. b	**2. a**	**2. a**	**2. d**	
3. d	**3. b**	**3. a**	**3. c**	
4. b	**4. c**	**4. d**	**4. c**	
5. a	**5. c**	**5. b**	**5. c**	
6. a	**6. d**	**6. c**	**6. b**	
7. b	**7. c**	**7. b**	**7. b**	
8. c	**8. b**	**8. a**	**8. c**	
9. c	**9. c**	**9. d**	**9. d**	
10. a	**10. c**	**10. b**	**10. b**	

Recommended Reading

Following is a list of books that you may want to consult for additional information for you and your students on the topics and concepts discussed in the text.

Making Successful Transitions

Fletcher, Anne. *Sober for Good.* Boston: Houghton Mifflin, 2001.

Gardner, Howard E. *Multiple Intelligences: The Theory in Practice.* New York: Basic Books, 1993.

Koch, Nadine S. and K. William Wasson. *The Transfer Student's Guide to the College Experience.* Boston: Houghton Mifflin Company, 2002.

Kolb, David A. *Experiential Learning: Experience As the Source of Learning and Development.* Englewood Cliffs, NJ: Financial Times Prentice Hall, 1984.

Light, Richard J. *Making the Most of College: Students Speak Their Minds.* Cambridge, MA: Harvard University Press, 2001.

Seligman, Marin E. *Learned Optimism: How to Change Your Mind and Your Life.* New York: Simon and Schuster, 1998.

Thinking Critically and Creatively

Adler, Mortimer J. *How to Read a Book.* New York: Simon & Schuster, 1987.

Engleberg, Isa, and Dianna Wynn. *Working in Groups: Communication Principles and Strategies.* Boston: Houghton Mifflin, 2003.

Facione, Peter. *Critical Thinking: What It Is and Why It Counts.* Millbrae, CA: California Academic Press, 1996.

Koestler, Arthur. *The Act of Creation.* New York: Dell, 1964.

Nalebuff, Barry, and Ian Ayres. *Why Not? How to Use Everyday Ingenuity to Solve Problems Big and Small.* Boston: Harvard Business School Press, 2003.

Nosich, Gerald M. *Learning to Think Things Through.* Upper Saddle River, NJ: Prentice-Hall, 2001.

Osborn, Alex F. *Applied Imagination.* New York: Scribner, 1979.

Paul, Dr. Richard, and Dr. Linda Elder. *The Miniature Guide for Those Who Teach on How to Improve Student Learning.* Dillon Beach, CA: Foundation for Critical Thinking, 2002.

Paul, Dr. Richard, and Dr. Linda Elder. *The Miniature Guide on How to Detect Media Bias and Propaganda.* Dillon Beach, CA: Foundation for Critical Thinking, 2003.

Ruggiero, Vincent Ryan. *Becoming a Critical Thinker*, 4/e. Boston: Houghton Mifflin, 2002.

Tracy, Brian. *Eat that Frog: 21 Great Ways to Stop Procrastinating and Get More Done in Less Time.* San Francisco: Berrett-Koehler Publishers, 2001.

Warmke, Clare, and Lisa Buchanan. *Idea Revolution: Guidelines and Prompts for Brainstorming Alone, in Groups, and with Clients.* Cincinnati: HOW Design Books, 2003.

White, Fred D. and Simone J. Billings. *The Well-Crafted Argument: A Guide and Reader.* Boston: Houghton Mifflin Company, 2002.

Planning to Succeed

Bolles, Richard Nelson. *What Color Is Your Parachute?* Berkeley, CA: Ten Speed Press, 2003.

Covey, Stephen R. *The Seven Habits of Highly Effective People: Restoring the Character Ethic.* New York: Simon & Schuster, 1989.

Covey, Stephen R. *First Things First.* New York: Simon & Schuster, 1994.

Ellis, Dave. *Creating Your Future: Five Steps to the Life of Your Dreams.* Boston: Houghton Mifflin, 1998.

Ellis, Dave, Stan Lankowitz, Ed Stupka, and Doug Taft. *Career Planning*, 3/e. Boston: Houghton Mifflin, 2003.
Greene, Susan D. and Melanie C. L. Martel. *The Ultimate Job Hunter's Guidebook*, 4/e. Boston: Houghton Mifflin Company, 2004.
Laekin, Alan. *Take Control of Your Time and Life.* New York: New American Library, 1973.
Lathrop, Richard. *Who's Hiring Who?* Berkeley, CA: Ten Speed Press, 1989.
Sapadin, Linda. *It's About Time – The Six Styles of Procrastination and How to Overcome Them.* New York: Penguin, 1997.
Scharf-Hunt, Diana, and Pam Hait. *Studying Smart: Time Management for College Students.* New York: HarperPerennial, 1990.
Winston, Stephanie. *Getting Organized.* New York: Warner, 1978.

Reading and Note-Taking with a Purpose

Adler, Mortimer, and Charles Van Doren. *How to Read a Book.* New York: Touchstone, 1972.
Ausubal, David. *The Psychology of Meaningful Verbal Learning.* New York: Grune & Stratton, 1963.
Barton, William A. *Outlining As a Study Procedure.* New York: Teachers College Columbia University, 1930.
Buzan, Tony. *Use Both Sides of Your Brain.* New York: Dutton, 1991.
Gilbart, Helen W. *Pathways: A Guide to Reading and Study Skills.* Boston: Houghton Mifflin, 1982.
Kesselman-Turk, Judi, and Franklynn Peterson. *Note-Taking Made Easy.* Madison, WI: University of Wisconsin Press, 2003.
Lewis, Jill. *Reading for Academic Success: Readings and Strategies*. Boston: Houghton Mifflin Company, 2002.
Lim, Phyllis L., and William Smalzer. *Noteworthy: Listening and Note-Taking Skills.* Pacific Grove, CA: Heinle & Heinle, 1990.
Pauk, Walter, and Ross J. Q. Owens. *How to Study in College*, 8/e. Boston: Houghton Mifflin, 2005.
Power, Brenda Miller. *Taking Note: Improving Your Observational Notetaking.* York, ME: Stenhouse Publishers, 1995.
Schoenbach, Ruth. *Reading for Understanding.* San Francisco: Jossey-Bass Publishers, 1999.

Building Memory and Test-Taking Skills

Brown, Alan C. *Maximizing Memory Power.* New York: Wiley, 1986.
Davis, Martha, Elizabeth Robbins Eshelman, and Matthew McKay. *Relaxation & Stress Reduction Workbook.* Oakland, CA: New Harbinger Publications, 1988.
Gordon, Barry, and Lisa Berger. *Intelligent Memory: Improve the Memory That Makes You Smarter.* New York: Viking, 2003.
Higbee, Kenneth L. *Your Memory: How It Works and How to Improve It.* Englewood Cliffs, NJ: Prentice-Hall, 1996.
Meyers, Judith N. *The Secrets of Taking Any Test.* New York: Learning Express, 2000.
Rozakis, Laurie. *Test Taking Strategies & Study Skills for the Utterly Confused.* New York: McGraw-Hill, 2003.
Schacter, Daniel. *The Seven Sins of Memory: How the Mind Forgets and Remembers.* Boston: Houghton Mifflin, 2001.
Wurman, Richard Saul. *Information Anxiety.* New York: Doubleday, 1989.

Developing and Presenting Ideas

Behrens, Laurence, and Leonard Rosen. *Writing and Reading Across the Curriculum.* New York: Longman, 2004.

Brown, David (Editor). *Ubiquitous Computing: The Universal Use of Computers on College Campuses.* Bolton, MA: Anker Publishing Company, 2003.
Carnegie, Dale. *The Quick and Easy Way to Effective Speaking.* New York: Pocket Books, 1962.
Cheney, Theodore. *Getting the Words Right: How to Revise, Edit, and Rewrite.* Cincinnati: Writer's Digest, 1983.
Elbow, Peter. *Writing with Power: Techniques for Mastering the Writing Process.* New York: Oxford University Press, 1981.
Engleberg, Isa and Ann Raimes. *Pocket Keys for Speakers*. Boston: Houghton Mifflin Company, 2004.
Gibaldi, Joseph. *MLA Handbook for Writers of Research Papers.* New York: Modern Language Association, 1999.
Goldberg, Natalie. *Writing Down the Bones: Freeing the Writer Within.* Boston: Shambahala, 1992.
Grice, George L., and John F. Skinner. *Mastering Public Speaking.* Boston: Pearson, 2004.
Motley, Michael T. *Overcoming Your Fear of Public Speaking: A Proven Method.* Boston: Houghton Mifflin, 1997.
Osborn, Michael and Susan Osborn. *Public Speaking*, 6/e. Boston: Houghton Mifflin Company, 2003.
Raimes, Ann. *Universal Keys for Writers.* Boston: Houghton Mifflin, 2004.
Shelton, Karla, and Todd McNeeley. *Virtual Communities Companion: Everything You Need to Know About Online Communities.* Albany, NY: Coriolis Group Books, 1997.
Strunk, William, and E. B. White. *The Elements of Style.* New York: Macmillan, 1979.
VanderMey, Randall, Verne Meyer, John Van Rys, Dave Kemper, and Pat Sebranek. *The College Writer: A Guide to Thinking, Writing, and Researching*. Boston: Houghton Mifflin Company, 2004.
Watkins, Ryan and Michael Corry. *E-Learning Companion: A Student's Guide to Online Success.* Boston: Houghton Mifflin Company, 2005.

Succeeding in Math and Science

Arem, Cynthia A. *Conquering Math Anxiety: A Self-Help Workbook.* Pacific Grove, CA: Brooks/Cole-Thomson Learning, 2003.
Burns, Marilyn. *Math: Facing an American Phobia.* Sausalito, CA: Math Solutions Publications, 1998.
Kogelman, Stanley, and Joseph Warren. *Mind Over Math.* New York: Dial Press, 1978.
Mallow, Jeffrey V. *Science Anxiety: Fear of Science and How to Overcome It.* New York: Thomond, 1986.
Nolting, Paul D. *Math Study Skills Workbook*, 2/e. Boston: Houghton Mifflin Company, 2005.
Tobias, Sheila. *Succeed with Math: Every Student's Guide to Conquering Math Anxiety.* New York: College Board, 1995.